Praise for Timur Shah

Weaving together the personal with the universal, Timur Shah combines self-exploration with timeless wisdom. The result is by turns playful and insightful and shines with original talent.

— Jason Elliot,
author of *An Unexpected Light*

Timur Shah's stories are by turns visceral, playful and challenging, provocatively injecting elements of the fantastic into our everyday world. This volume shows a lively, clever mind at work: a creative talent to watch for the future.

— Jane Johnson,
author of *Court of Lions*

At once personal yet universal, learned yet not showy, original yet traditional... Beautifully written, attractively thoughtful, and achingly honest.

— Fitzroy Morrissey,
author of *A Short History of Arab Thought*

Timur Shah is a highly original writer.

— James Von Leyden,
author of *Last Boat From Tangier*

Timur Shah writes with a lively, thoughtful and accomplished new voice, bringing fresh resonance and personal perspective.
– Fiona Valpy,
author of *The Storyteller of Casablanca*

From a distinguished family of storytellers and writers, an exciting new voice has emerged.
– Richard Hamilton,
author of *The Last Storytellers*

A preternaturally sensitive young writer who finds his voice – his voices – to counter the isolation and meaninglessness of our age.
– Josh Shoemake,
author of Tangier: *A Literary Guide for Travellers*

Startlingly honest confessional essays about his insecurities, and their significance for him and for humanity in general.
– Nigel Hinton,
author of *Ship of Ghosts*

A uniquely kaleidoscopic and ambitious vision ranging across millennia.
– Michael Moran,
author of *Beyond the Coral Sea*

In this lovely first collection, Timur Shah keeps the embers of our oldest stories glowing and reminds us that the value we find in ourselves (and what we can do) gives us hope and strength in a world not designed to serve our needs, preferences, or ideals.

— Mark Salzman,
author of *Iron & Silk*

A remarkable and highly imaginative book from a dynamic young thinker and storyteller. I very much hope he has others on the way.

— JonArno Lawson,
author of *Footpath Flowers*

Whether the setting is Ogygia, Antarctica or Tottenham Court Road, Timur Shah sends down buckets into the deepest wells of humankind's myths, and draws fresh stories and sparkling morals. Could there, for example, be an apter legend for the age of social media and its angsts than that of Narcissus and Echo?

'By adding to stories,' Timur writes, 'we are using them the way they were meant to be used.' He is right, and he has all the assets to add yet more, for us and for audiences to come.

— Tim Mackintosh-Smith,
author of *Travels with a Tangerine*

In a strikingly original blend of scholarship and imagination, *An Ordered Experience* summons up some of the worlds great mythic pantheons and their stories and gives them new and personal meanings in modern life, thereby transforming doubt and failure into a literary triumph.

– Robert Irwin,
author of *The Arabian Nights: A Companion*

A mercurial and erudite medley of epic retellings, short stories and literary analysis that playfully and poignantly underlines the endless adaptability of some of the world's greatest myths.

– Nick Jubber,
author of *The Fairy Tellers*

A tour de force full of invention, interest and fine writing, Timur Shah is a fascinating young writer of great promise and potential.

– Robert Twigger,
author of *Angry White Pyjamas*

From a distinguished family of storytellers and writers, an exciting new voice has emerged.

This is a wonderfully rich and quirky collection of short stories. Timur Shah has dipped into ancient mythology and folk tales, reworked them and turned them on their head. I was struck by the original take on old stories, from a chance encounter between Odysseus and Achilles in Hades, to a scientist conducting research in Antarctica who loses an eyeball, to a nervous university student who receives invaluable advice from Dionysus, to eating salad with Zeus, this is a vibrant mix of the bizarre and the fabulous.

– Richard Hamilton,
author of *The Last Storytellers*

A sincere, hopeful, and heartfelt blend of essay and fiction by a preternaturally sensitive young writer who finds his voice – his voices – by engaging with classic myths, calmly determined to find the antidotes to the isolation and meaninglessness of our age.

– Josh Shoemake,
author of *Tangier: A Literary Guide for Travellers*

Timur Shah's book is an extraordinary and fascinating mixture: there are startlingly honest confessional essays about his insecurities, ruminations on myths and legends and their significance for him and for humanity in general, and a series of short stories into which the myths and legends seep. What is apparent throughout these diverse styles is that Shah, despite his own doubts about the fact, is a real writer. This is a terrific debut.

– Nigel Hinton,
author of *Ship of Ghosts*

A uniquely kaleidoscopic and ambitious vision ranging across millennia connecting profound ancient myths to our transformed technological present.

– Michael Moran,
author of *Beyond the Coral Sea*

This is an intriguing, poised, and creative debut from someone who truly understands the power and value of myth.

– Bijan Omrani,
author of *Caesar's Footprints*

Infinite
Internal
Monologue

Infinite
Internal
Monologue

TIMUR SHAH

The Scheherazade Foundation CIC
85 Great Portland Street
London
W1W 7LT
United Kingdom

www.SF.Charity
info@SF.Charity

First published by The Scheherazade Foundation CIC, 2025

INFINITE INTERNAL MONOLOGUE

© TIMUR SHAH

TimurShah.com

Timur Shah asserts the right to be identified as the Author of the Work
in accordance with the Copyright, Designs and Patents Act 1988.
A CIP catalogue record for this title is available from the British Library.

ISBN 978-1-915311-66-5

For the version of myself that wrote this book.

These are the days that must happen to you.

Walt Whitman

Contents

Cameraman on the Street

To see is to forget the name of the thing one sees.

Paul Valéry

I FEEL POCKETS OF CONTROLLED CHAOS.

A city that belongs to everyone and, increasingly, to nobody. One calling simultaneously for individual expression and constraints wherever they could be managed. The ideal of this was, to me, the simplicity of spaces between buildings.

This ranged from none at all, to the handful of feet, to the blocks I had been expecting. Those gaps are the unaccounted-for or otherwise-owned spaces that separate brick and steel and time, and add a breath – or none – between styles and moments and singular visions for the sky.

I am struck – as I constantly appear to be – by the scale of it all.

By the scale of difference.

It's a scale that vanishes with degrees. The moment I look up in this city, no matter by how much, I'm treated to monuments of human greatness and achievement that, in reality, only succeed in making me feel as small as I wish I weren't.

But there is a balance to things.

Skyscraper and human alike share the same entropic, Ozymandian fate in this city.

I walk fast – as everyone does here – down the great gaps of avenues.

Every couple of hundred feet, we are treated to a running expanse, to time height and scale and chrome and glass and rebar and time once again, stretching for tens of dozens of numbers. The sheer mass of the Chrysler building, its head peeking in the distance downtown, looking like a model out of a children's toy box.

Marching as I am down one of the avenues, I weave my way through food delivery drivers huddled outside one of the chrome-and-glass castles, separate but somehow united in their collective representation as a whole against the thirty-somethings with well-coiffed hair who would soon retrieve their salads, burgers, or burrito bowls.

The building in which they work seems to be made of entire buildings of its own, with burnished architectural struts twice as tall as the synagogue just one block north.

Spaces and places of worship here seem to be the few instances in this city of ingenuity and breadth focused down into itself, distinguishing themselves from the expanse of the heavens. It's a lovely mass of dark pink stone, tessellating in a pattern I could not quite grasp.

Religion is full of those patterns.

A woman eats her takeout on the steps of the synagogue, listening to whatever she's listening to.

In my head, it's a Dire Straits album; in hers, it's probably a podcast. An unhoused man puts on a stained tartan shirt further down the steps. The lines and roundedness that make up the building's holy mass, the angles and circles that communicate a unique history in a city rife with it, familiar to those who ought to be familiar with it.

On another avenue, of dizzying length and individual significance, stand delicately carved, statuesque and marble and tile pillars of a church. It bears on its outside a sign welcoming those that exist outside of its preaching in thought, seeking an expansion of the faith it, as a building, represents.

Circling back, I see the fifty stars and however many stripes it is that catch the light as bumper stickers, that show their wrinkles as they flap lightly in the air, that denote language and accessibility in a city where such warnings are needed, where they're baked into its identity.

Everywhere, somebody's old is somebody's new.

New York is a city that, in its short time frame of existence, has expanded outwards, inwards, and upwards.

And downwards, too.

Discovering that underworld entails an adventure down the steps, where the wet heat and the scent of the sweat of millions and their machines hastens from the vents above.

Through my own disordered descriptions, I strain to make sense of places.

As much as I can, I endeavour to let experience exist within me unmarred by such sense. Such experience, though, is all too valuable in my conception of that sense. My judgements, given their own unfortunate point of conception, are all too often concerned with the self.

Despite my philosophical objections, the translation of my experiences into something semi-tangible is the first step in what has come to be my regular invocation of a posteriori reasoning.

So, yes, while I waste my time admiring incomprehensible sentences of which the preceding one is a prime example, it's an amusing pastime to work through such experiences. I consider the process to be similar, in a way, to photography.

I take a picture with a film camera because I'm cool and retro, the scene hitting the film as it and my own settings try their best to make it look good.

Then, maybe the viewfinder doesn't look through the lens, or maybe I forgot to adjust the focus. What if I used the wrong film stock for that kind of light? What if the subject is blurred, or simply unexciting?

I don't care. At least, I try not to care.

In any case, I don't believe in the intentionally perfect picture.

Even if I could believe in it, though, I wouldn't want to.

What a dull existence that would be, letting go of that potential, the spontaneity I am otherwise too often without. That piece above, the description I summoned from somewhere unreliable within me, is the post-processing of it all.

It is the attempt to salvage what is fading or what faded from the start, and retain and reiterate its significance. Each experience is inescapably an inward reflection, a city of massive intricate and ineffable detail inside me.

Those experiences of New York seeped in through my lens over six months ago now, and I cherish that I've been able to reimagine them. Not for the me of that time, who would have poked holes in my story or have been indifferent in diminishing its importance, but for me now. They may go back to being just details again, but at this moment, I've captured a time for myself.

So, indulge me.

Let me appreciate a little, a little while longer.

Credo

I'm a pessimist because of intelligence,
but an optimist because of will.

Antonio Gramsci

It's nice to be nice to myself.

To afford my infinite internal monologue the benefit of the doubt.

Even in my more positive moods and moments, conjuring a little more of that positivity and directing it inwards has not been a consistent forte of mine.

Instead, I hold on to that warm, glowing feeling in a tight clump inside, until my internal noticing power changes back from emotion to reason, and that inexplicable ball of concentrated joy unceremoniously dissipates.

In this little book, I am at serious risk of finding different ways to write about and reason through what are, ostensibly, the same quandaries that govern my mind… quandaries that can broadly fall under 'things I think too much about' and 'things I've grown used to not thinking enough about'.

And, as this and that last sentence suggest, the iterations that come will always be more convoluted and crammed with clauses than their precedents.

Increasingly still, it's through steps like this that I most reliably come to know myself.

Ever since I learned they could make me feel how someone else wanted to make me feel, I have loved stories – stories in the multitude of forms they take.

So, I have long been satisfied, and even pleased, when meaningful story and character trajectories present themselves in reference to my own experience of existence. Such simplistic and not-quite-whole descriptors make more sense to me than most other things I encounter on my path to self-recognition, and I encounter them in this space.

With words, and with writing.

In this medium, where ideas are formed and breathed into unique life, novelty in the mind is a welcome by-product. Words placed unthinkingly or accidentally that fit better than what was intended, putting a thought simply, putting a thought in a thousand words, discovering patterns in what has finally been granted reality.

These have been the ways in which I grow.

I am aware that this space is one in which change is fostered, solely because it remains my only real outlet. All the people in my life are subject to different, not-quite-whole versions of myself, interacting with me when I'm less than the sum of my parts.

It is a constant here.

The individual who is writing and being defined by these words is a knowing fraction of an unknowing but complete person. But here is where I come the closest to that mythical entirety of self. In this world, meaning is secondary to the choice and order of words, but it is not absent.

The meaning that arises here is rarely whole, or wholly true.

If enough of it works, that's good enough for me. If there is a morsel of meaning to which I can relate, or with which I can comfort or even explain myself, I consider that a success.

My clichéd search for meaning sees me working to locate

the puzzle pieces making up characters I see – both fictional and real. With that come desperate efforts to jam them into my own puzzle, knowing full well they're the wrong shape and belong to a completely different picture.

But all the same, they are from a complete picture. I'm short on answers and puzzle pieces of my own, and am comfortable admitting to gaps in social skills and experience.

I am constantly on the lookout for anything that looks like it might fit.

It's something I first noticed when a friend was telling me how they strongly related to a character in a TV show we both liked.

I'd felt the same connection, about the same character. But when I asked what it was about the character that made them feel they could relate, I received an answer that implied a definition of 'relating to' that I had myself not been using.

Deconstructing what kind of definition my own feeling was attached to was the first step in recognising that I form those kinds of relationships differently. In relating to something, I seek a solution or a guide for my own life as opposed to a simple appreciation for a shared trait.

The examples highlight more than just a problem. They show the problem in context – or even in solution; two matching puzzle pieces I am sorely missing. Noticing I have an issue, or even a goal, in common with someone else rouses me about getting to see the way in which they dealt with it.

How inconsistent this all is, and how frustrating.

Some of these unrelated puzzle pieces work better than others. I often find myself trying to shoehorn my own experiences into others' tales of woe, adjusting the way I feel to fit in with what they're saying. My hope is that whatever conclusion or peace they have reached is one that I, too, might achieve by replicating the effort and the experiences of their solutions.

Exasperating though it may be, it's been a relief to see that a subtlety of the reverse can be true as well. Ted Lasso, a favourite show of mine, champions and revolves around the simple concept that inspires those associated with the fictional AFC Richmond.

Believe.

I have always registered the sentiment, enjoying its use in the show's character development and drama. But the appreciation I held for it seemed to exist in a plane separate from the introspective one I tend to inhabit.

My guess for why that is would be that such introspection in that context would repudiate a facet of my thinking with which I've become too comfortable.

My act of belief is one I remain too aware of as being an 'act'.

Columnist George F. Will wrote: 'The nice part about being a pessimist is that you are constantly being either proven right or pleasantly surprised.'

It's an optimistic view on pessimism that's one of two important ideals that I use to justify my own. The other is a deep-rooted conviction that the criticisms I maintain about myself come as a result of such a logical series of conclusions that they couldn't be anything but right. To be able to dismiss that way of thinking, as well as its defence, is such a relief.

Expecting anything better is the misplaced hope of delusion.

I have a lot of mental barriers yet to work through, most of which being at least as resolute as my deluded optimism once was.

Returning to the beginning, though: it's nice to be nice to myself.

That's one way through which I can start to dismantle the high status I so naturally employ to extol both my insecurities and negativity. Within themselves they contain an unpleasantness, sure, but they do also offer a kind of cruel comfort. Just enough of it to make thinking past it not seem a worthy venture.

So, proof as this whole piece has been of my ability to allow for some unfounded optimism – some *belief* – in my life, it also demonstrates something much more simple, and reassuring.

I am as many solutions as I am problems. That, and my apparent hatred of brevity.

As long as I am me, though, the hitches and hurdles don't stand a chance.

Just don't tell them I said that.

Think Fast

I would my horse had the speed of your tongue.

William Shakespeare, *Much Ado About Nothing*

PEOPLE DON'T TALK like they do in the movies, which really bums me out.

Obscure political and pop culture references don't regularly show up to add flavour to a verbal sparring match. People are, in fact, rather reluctant to refer to conversations as 'verbal sparring matches'. Those perfect witty one-liners are rare, and I have yet to live the undeniable joy of someone setting me up for the perfect, movie-esque, one-two joke and call-back.

Unfortunately, such movies, and a great many TV shows, are the medium through which I developed my own style of thinking. As such, and as a vessel for a myriad of cultural deep-cuts from cinema, television, and literature, that style of thinking is condemned to remain within me. More and more, my sense is that it will never be realised in fancy, rapid-fire exchanges of patter or banter.

Now, on to the *why* of it all.

Sure, no one really talks like that, but why not?

Why am I denied this reality? Why can't I live in the joy of such repartee?

While I'm sure there are a number of contributing factors, the primary one I have landed on is the prevalence in modern life of phatic vernacular – i.e. the exchange of vacuous pleasantries which dominate so much of our interaction with others.

The 'nice weather we're having', combined with the 'you alright?', and 'how's it going?' A significant portion of our speech is devoted to carrying forward the argot of social interaction – sidelining to an extent genuinely interrogative or information-conveying material.

If I may borrow a reference from a Simon and Garfunkel song older than my parents, much of life today is occupied by 'people talking without speaking'.

This observation is not one with which I can take issue for risk of venturing too far towards hypocrisy. Yes, in the land of those conversing for the sake of conversing, I am recognised for my proficiency.

The point is, the relatively small part of my day spent in conversation with people is rarely used in an informationally constructive way. Given my disinclination to begin socialising with strangers, the occasions on which I find myself in that situation are populated with the same phatic expressions, continued and unending volleys of emptiness.

Believe me – it takes effort, and even skill, to take interest in someone's life, asking meaningful questions and providing equally meaningful follow-ups.

What I do, on the other hand, is achieved with nothing more than repetition. Some might say practice, but I wouldn't presume to go that far. It turns out that there are only so many ways to answer the question 'how's your day going?', and even fewer ways to feign interest in others' answers.

All of this comes at a cost of great pain to me.

I half-arse my way through most conversations, relying on instinct and experience more than an actual interest, and I am sure the same is true for most people I encounter. Juxtapose this against the movies and shows I referred to at the start – the ones with the witty and perfectly timed dialogue – and you begin wondering why this deficiency still seems so inescapable.

The ill-fated fork in my path from the masses is that I seem to be the rare kind of viewer who perceives those scenes, those exchanges, as more than mere entertainment.

For me, it's nothing short of aspirational.

But it remains the way I compose my thoughts. I think in grand speeches, in biting insults, and in the kind of backtalk only a television writer in the mid-to-late nineties would see fit to put in front of an audience.

It's a curse, albeit a fun one.

When it comes to specific zeitgeists of the second half of the twentieth century, the gaps in my knowledge have been filled in by this dialogue. Indeed, I'm a treasure trove of obscure, largely irrelevant information.

Who knew that watching decades of movies out of Hollywood would teach me a thing or two or three thousand about its country's turns of phrase, and simultaneously banal and scandalous politics?

It's fun, but an inescapably lonely kind of fun.

Even if I did possess the glorious ability to mimic those speech patterns and employ them in my own day-to-day life, the efficacy of spewing out references from political or cultural history is greatly diminished. This is, in part, due to the sheer obscurity of these once societal touchstones, combined with the fact that speaking in these references is not something that most people are ready to encounter in casual (or heated, for that matter) conversation.

Therein lies the tragedy of it all.

I cannot speak to whether this striking art form *should* be sought after in real life or emulated in actual conversations, but I know that one has no hope of doing so on their own. Both a boon and a bane of this kind of dialogue's nature is its mutual interactivity. Not only is it not fun for one to do this on their own, but doing so fails to meet the criteria of what one is trying to achieve.

One of my favourite screenwriters, Aaron Sorkin, is an archetypal master of this type of writing and, I would submit, one of its foremost progenitors. Above the writing, there is something conceptual, about a certain type of scene that he writes, that I love.

Simply put, it's that almost every time two people are arguing about something, with no pauses between their exchanges and perfect rhythm to their flowing phrases, both of them are correct. Be they broadcast journalists, baseball scouts, or budding entrepreneurs, they don't debate the sheer logics of a case.

Instead, it's the morality that's up in the air.

So, yes, as much as I do aspire to the dialogue whose praises I have sung, whose reality I regularly fail to manifest, and whose precise sound I always have echoing in my ears throughout my waking hours, dawn until dusk, it's more often the actual situation I appreciate.

It's subtextual and nuanced, but also plain to see and eminently solvable.

Situations just don't manifest and behave like that in the real world.

Neither do they transpire as they do in a Sorkin-esque or Soderbergh-esque or *Gilmore Girls*-esque kind of choreographed reality.

I may have settled for the one I'm living in, but I'm not entirely satisfied yet.

Cogito

I did then what I knew how to do.
Now that I know better, I do better.

Maya Angelou

AT THIS MOMENT, I know only a fraction of what I am going to know.

I love that notion, aside from the fact that it comes close to making me face mortal fear.

To be honest, though, I only really know part of what I know right now. You see, in my mind, knowledge and assorted information rarely interact.

Allow me to run an analogy by you.

I hope I don't get carried away.

Imagine a hard drive.

Not entirely different, conceptually, from the over-engineered storage devices that are, essentially, our brains. Every time I try to explain how my brain stores and retrieves data, I visualise it as a computer. Simplistic though this may seem, simple is my mind's chosen avenue of thought-production. Perhaps the result is the father of the thought in this instance. I've become so accustomed to thinking about and using this analogy that I have no way of knowing how much it still applies, or indeed, how much it ever really did.

Now for a disclaimer of sorts:

By nature, I am self-centred.

It's not that I find it difficult to conceptualise other people's minds or ways of thinking – but rather that I haven't ever tried to.

Any statement I make about myself which applies to you

or other people is made out of sheer ignorance. I justify this to myself as being an apathetic and mild flavour of solipsism.

There is more still to be disclaimed.

Not only am I almost entirely incapable of extrapolating my general state of consciousness onto others, but I cannot trust my perception of that state of consciousness at all. As with the hard drive analogy, it changes regularly to whatever dumbed-down rationalisation makes the most sense to me at that moment in time.

Aaron Sorkin said about writing dialogue that 'What the words sound like is as important to [him] as what the words mean.' I think that any meaning in my work is largely accidental and, though welcome, isn't a priority of mine.

It's for this reason that I have long struggled to express myself through poetry, despite a sincere desire to. It has taken understanding this part of myself to slip out of the comforting walls of rhyme. I learned how to use my favourite collections of sounds and expressive imagery to contribute to the mood, carrying through at least some of that self-expression without having to rely too heavily on the words – their meanings, or the order in which I arrange them.

Instead of describing, I am attempting to evoke ideas and feelings.

With any luck, I'll return to the hard drive plot at a later point.

After all, there is a lot more to be said on the subject of my relationship to words and my writing. I can write at length about my slow willingness to let an untrue, albeit catchy, descriptor of myself go. Part of it is a reluctance to acknowledge the truth concealed behind it, but it is in equal measure about something else the words represented – my thoughts.

One of my greatest fears is that I'm not as smart as I believe I am. So here we find another pretty descriptor that's held on as truth so far.

How I believe that has manifested in myself is by using long words and even longer sentences in writing and in my internal thoughts. This is done, I suppose, to allow criticism or even mere judgements of the former to credibly assess the quality of the latter.

But there's a dangerous component to all of this, pertaining to the particular wording of that fear. The 'as I believe I am' part is as meek a reference as I can make to the self-aggrandising truth of my ego. Unless presently compared to work I consider to be better, my own stands out as clever and well written.

The ego that is so quick to place my writing on so high a pedestal is also why my fear has gone so far unchallenged. In that effort to pass criticisms of my work onto the thoughts that spawned it all, I have so far been stuck at the hurdle of accepting criticism. Only really on a macro scale, on the subject of ideas and the order in which I'm communicating them, do I ever really register criticism as possibly being valid.

In every other case, when I know those words in that order are exactly what I meant, and I like them, there is little that can be done to convince me otherwise. This point applies less when I'm writing fiction, because there is a filter between thought and writing, and a lovely lack of that blind faith in the product.

Regardless, that fault in my thinking has the convenient result of not often encountering any reasonable opposition. Perhaps it is a mental defence mechanism, in which case my brain knows where to draw the line in appraisals of my work, lest they call into question the more deep-rooted and intrinsic components of my psyche.

I'm not really sure how I got here, but I seem to have gone from what was a discussion about the way I think and the way my brain-hard-drive stores memories, to a deconstruction of how much my writing reflects the way I think, ending with a defence of intellectualism and elongated words and sentences such as these, citing some innate, half-reasoned instinct for cerebral self-preservation.

Only now has it occurred to me that breaking down my propensity for pithy statements about myself is itself contributing to the problem, in a way. Indulging my thoughts with permanence is a slippery, near-incomprehensible slope. But it's also tricky to attempt an understanding of my own knowledge at all, if only because the process is itself constrained by what I already know.

Unfortunately, what I know is most usually what is comfortable to know, and that which seems to require too much effort to call into question. I am a self-important, semantically certain, semi-solipsistic serpent eating my own tail, an *ouroboros* drawing conclusions from 'facts', and facts from 'conclusions'.

Left to my own devices, my thoughts, my words, are my greatest enemy.

But don't they sound good?

Situational Discomfort

Authority works only when people obey.

Harjeet Khanduja

WELCOME to *Timur Has a Complicated Relationship With…*™, the sadly introspective game show that absolutely no one is talking about.

First, we'd like to extend our gratitude to a man without whom none of this would be possible, a man whose problems and opinions are too many to enumerate. Please, give a big round of applause for Timur!

Go on, feed his ego!

Well, folks, we all know how the game works, so let's get started.

Timur, why don't you go ahead and…

SPIN…THAT…WHEEL!

We've got a lot of great options tonight, and some old favourites he might return to.

Okay, it's slowing down – what will it be this time?

Friendship, motivation, travel, socialising, social events, sociability?

Maybe we'll even finally find out why he can't stand airplane food.

Oh! It looks like a topic has been reached, and it's bound to be another snoozefest of an episode.

There's no point delaying any longer, it's time to hear why Timur has a complicated relationship with… authority!

Take it away, Timur!

Where should I begin?

Does this piece have a thesis? Two very good questions, and the answer to both is a confident and resounding 'I don't know'. You see, authority is something I fear and something I lack. Despite both of those seemingly negative points, I have long debated with myself whether either would be good for me, or might even be something I want.

I have always been what a goody two-shoes might describe as a 'wannabe goody two-shoes'. My dread of authority, then, when characterised more as an intense dislike, begins to show parallels with my aversion to any situational discomfort at all.

The 'wannabe' part comes from this position being that of the least resistance. In almost all the examples I can think of, any activity that involved the risk of my getting in trouble had a high, high bar of guaranteed fun to first be reached.

The overwhelming majority of these relevant examples are, alas, the furthest thing from exciting. Given most of my life before this moment has been spent in some version of a scholastic environment, those examples comprise my compulsive need to follow instructions given to me.

I can count on one hand the number of times I handed in a piece of homework late. This compulsion did not extend to ensuring any degree of quality for that work. In fact, praise was rarely sought, and black marks on my academic record weren't necessarily avoided.

I aimed as high as I was asked, with as much effort as I could summon at that moment in time. What I steered clear of was anything that put me in those aforementioned uncomfortable situations.

The authority figures I appreciated most during my time at school were those with whom errors were not dwelled upon. It spawned relationships I can now recognise as constructive because they meant I would be more willing to do interesting things which didn't guarantee success. Those superiors of whom I harboured a low opinion viewed failures as opportunities for deep character reflection.

I'm grateful that it is the low stakes that I have encountered the most – god knows I'll be a wreck whenever I'm so unlucky as to meet authority figures out in the big wide world, and not know which kind I'll be encountering until it's too late.

On to the authority I myself inhabit.

I simply have none.

Countless self-help books and their authors are wont to ascribe authority to confidence or charisma or any number of other unfortunately idealistic 'ideals', and they may be right. I don't know what boon I lack, or what deficiency I possess, that has carried forward the fact that I have never held any degree of authority.

Even in situations when it would have been to my advantage, such as being in a position of authority over others, nothing – not even threats of punishment – helped me in any way.

Kids don't respect me, and I respect that.

If I was resorting to fear-based authority – and I was – I'm relieved they didn't take me seriously. And therein lies a complication I find in my relationship with authority.

No, the show's not over. Yes, I know I've said the catchphrase, but I haven't made my point yet.

I don't know if I'm quite cut out for the authority game. In the first part of this chapter, I dissected my fear of authority until all that remained was something I've known about for a while already – I can't stand awkward social situations. That's a significant weapon in authority's arsenal, but it isn't the whole deal. I'm still no truant, nor likely to enter my recalcitrant era any time soon, but I am by no means aspiring to their opposites.

I am, I suppose, relatively content with the fact that is my inability to command any amount of authority. The last thing the world needs right now is someone with the general sentiment that they should be important, in an important role.

I am, to an extent, the former, but count my lucky stars I'm not the latter.

In this age, most of those in power seem to be some form of that unpleasant combination. In my life, authority and the power it often affords has been at its most effective and agreeable when said power is rarely wielded. Those who know more but don't belittle those who don't – those who know little but are actually open to learning.

Christopher Hitchens once described 'one of the beginnings of human emancipation [as being] the ability to laugh at authority'. I would extend that definition to include laughing with. The most inspiring authority figures I've encountered have been afforded such esteem in my mind by alleviating the awkwardness and power imbalance their situation imparts.

A teacher who treats their students like peers.

Pretend this sentence is an equally relevant example, as I cannot stress how little experience I have yet had in the big, wide world.

This show (piece) was filmed (written) in front of (while occasionally thinking about) a live studio audience.

Home, Grown

How often have I lain beneath rain
on a strange roof, thinking of home.

William Faulkner

THE FIRST SUBSTANTIAL purchase I'm going to make in my life is a house.

A house in a big city.

A city in which I understand the goings-on, and can be understood.

I don't want a car – at least, I don't want one any time soon. I tend to find the alternatives – public transport, trains, and plain walking – more than worthy substitutes.

No, it's to be a house, or a flat, or a studio, or an apartment, or whatever vessel feels meaningful in my larger search for a home.

Travel, in general, is another grand expenditure in which I'm willing to partake less to help conclude this search. In the process of travelling, one does place a greater value upon the experience, but it is one, I find, that makes what has been missing all the more appreciated and fulfilling.

To know where my clothes, my chargers, my dirty laundry, my books, and souvenirs fit in my suitcase for a weekend – or even a month-long stretch – is an experience perfectly pleasant in its own right.

It is made all the more pleasant, though, when that knowledge is paired with knowing where my souvenirs, my books, my dirty laundry, my chargers and clothes can return to when they and I converge on that ever-distant status quo. A trajectory entering a more familiar state.

Travel – and brevity, it would seem – can wait.

At least, until a certain condition is met – a home for my stuff, and for me.

So, what of other ways to spend money that can be expected or dreamt of by a burgeoning young man, such as myself?

Tech? Sure, a symptom of the time and of my upbringing, has been an awareness of all that's new and exciting and seen-to-be-believed in the world of tech. More often than not, and to a degree about which I have grown steadily less uncomfortable, I have given in to the promises of the cool – both emotionally and fiscally. For the last few years, though, I have been trying to chip away at that mindset, if not for its financial burden than the lack of follow-through those promises are liable to possess.

In the wake of such a style of thinking, what has seeped in through its cracks is the far less mentally taxing 'set it and forget it' doctrine. More or less, spend in a way that will deliver the product I expect, while best delaying the seemingly inevitable repeat of expense.

There is similarity here to the 'Boots Theory' Terry Pratchett suggests in his *Discworld* book, *Men at Arms*. His example works more to emphasise the economic burden placed on those in poverty, but I have co-opted a fraction of the following to help make sense of my fortunate position:

An excellent pair of boots costs $50.

For a rich man, the product is well worth the price, but for someone making $38 dollars a month, such an expense is impractical, if not entirely unconscionable. So, the salary man must instead opt for the $10 boots, the boots that, comparatively, are scarcely worth the cardboard soles they boast. The cheaper boots will break, will dissolve and disintegrate over little time, necessitating their owner buy just one more pair.

They will do it again.

The excellent boots will fare fine.

Their owner will replace them ten or so years down the line, by which time the salary man will have spent twice what the rich man paid, and for an inferior product and experience.

I'll admit, the portion I mentioned I extract from that theory is a very small part of it, but it's something I still thought worth sharing in entirety, if only to do one of my favourite things in the world: make myself feel bad for systemic, socio-economic unfairness over which I have no powers beyond the observational.

Before I briefly lost it, the point was that value is something I'm learning to see as a long term instead of a momentary idea. I do realise Pratchett's point was to comment on the injustice of a system that causes being poor to be so expensive.

This makes my attempt to draw some mild consumerist message out of it rather incurious and ignorant. So, I only hope that my reading of it in this instance as a tangential lesson about the relationship between value and quality doesn't appear too misplaced.

I am fortunate enough to be able to afford the $50 boots, but I, too, want (in this example and extrapolated to the real world) better boots to be cheaper and cheaper boots to be better. And for the value of the worker to be more emphasised and acknowledged and rewarded in society.

Forgive me, I'm on a preachy-Pratchett tangent.

Vive la révolution!

What else?

Next in the roadblocks I have placed in and must remove from my path is the entire history of property ownership in developed nations. In countries like the United States (and to a similar degree, the UK), it's a generally understood and evidence-based fact that younger populations cannot, and will never be able to, afford a home of their own.

Given that the majority of property belongs to those above the age of forty, and the rising disparities between supply and demand, it doesn't take an economic mind to recognise that home ownership is simply not a realistic prospect for those older than me – and least of all, my peers – to expect. It is a choice slowly ceasing to exist.

So, where does that leave me?

It does seem rather final a hurdle to encounter, and it definitely speaks to a societal wrong that needs to be addressed, but are there any patches I can stitch onto this moth-bitten quilt of an aspiration?

I hope so.

I don't know what will occupy me in my time to come. I may be a writer, or a version of it in a parallel industry, or something completely unrelated. Whatever it is, I don't foresee a hefty income by any means, so where should I start cutting corners?

Let's revisit some of those expectations and hopes from the start.

A house – perhaps.

I may have been closer to something with the more modest alternatives I listed, so let's call this a fluid variable – I'm keeping flats, for example, very much on the table. A big city? Hmm. That might be a bit trickier. I know what I was getting at, with the sense of connectedness and completeness I feel in a metropolis, but choosing it would force me to address factors of the real world I've been fortunate enough to put aside until now.

A place where I understand things and can make myself understood – yes! I'm finally onto something here. Think big, branch out. Learn to get comfortable with a language, and see at least one new map unlocked in the video game of my mind.

This is where I will make a home.

Screw finding one, I'll build a home for myself.

Even years from actually doing this, I'm stoked – I see it. And, for a while now, I've felt as though I need it. There's a recipe in front of me, for something I've known for a while that I'll love, and it calls for dozens of ingredients.

Some, such as a sense of permanence, I'll have to include for myself, some I'll omit entirely, and I'll improvise for the rest – I can make it work. I'll throw together a meal, a home, the mixed metaphor about which I feel palpable enthusiasm as I write this, and reach it, the next checkpoint at which I hope to arrive. I'm hungry.

Let's Get Critical

When the critic has said everything in his power about a literary text, he has still said nothing; for the very existence of literature implies that it cannot be replaced by non-literature.

Tzvetan Todorov

A BETTER ESSAY about criticism might start with a brief history of it.

But this is not that essay.

I'm not going to begin with that kind of discussion because it seems like far too broad a subject to research (I don't want to) and, equally, not one on which I think I would be able to thoughtfully comment (I really, really don't want to).

But one need not have studied the concept of criticism to foster opinions – and boy do I have opinions. They seem to be half the thoughts I have. If we're lucky, I may be able to sway some of those from opinion-form to well-reasoned, cogent points.

Criticism is, on the whole, an inescapable part of the creative-productive process, should that product be shown to at least one other person.

Did you paint a painting? Boom – *get criticised.*

Did you write a poem? You guessed it – *criticised!*

Did you fax over the latest budget reports to your boss? *Criticised – and in the year 1993, probably.*

It exists in our relationships, too – from friends and significant others who might find aspects of our behaviour challenging.

It's everywhere. Yay.

But you know all of this already.

So, why, you may be asking, am I spelling out the obvious?

The duality of both my critical and criticised selves has, over the course of undertaking projects such as this, been a prominent feature in my life.

Admittedly, the critical side rarely takes a day, let alone an hour, off. But the sudden presence of a volume of work – personal work – has introduced a heightened sense of being criticised.

While I am aware that 'criticisms' aren't necessarily damaging, and can sometimes be constructive, I am going to treat that specific iteration of the word primarily with reference to its negative connotation.

Criticisms of my work interest me because, unlike when they are used to pick away at my behaviour or social misgivings, those aimed at something I intentionally produced tend to bother me very little. They don't change any of my opinions as they pertain to what I've made, but instead contribute to those I form about the critic.

Simply put, I am aware of the deficiencies in my work, just as I am of the strengths.

As uncomprehending as it sounds – and likely is – I know the areas in which I can improve, and I know how very many of them there are. I know when I don't like the way dialogue sounds; or when I used the same word twice in one paragraph; or when I feel it all lacks something I was unable to articulate, or to include in a first draft.

Constructive criticisms of my work, I love.

I take great pleasure when an editor is able to resolve those deficiencies of which I am aware, because the most

I can really summon from myself is dissatisfaction. The conversion of those feelings into tangible ways to improve my work is the editorial equivalent of someone scratching an itch I can't myself reach.

Unfortunately, my inherent rejection of criticism carries over to the constructive side as well. It is invaluable to be able to distinguish within the pile of well-intentioned improvements the ones I believe are suited to my work; and it is a process both personal and impossible for me to convincingly explain.

The resident critic within me works within a completely unrelated realm.

He offers empty platitudes in order to spare feelings. He doesn't know what he's talking about with anything besides writing (and even then, his knowledge is pretty iffy), and so he isn't especially qualified to supply much more than general sentiment. Behaviourally speaking, he's infuriatingly pedantic. Did you misquote a fact, or use an incorrect plural, or say 'irregardless'?

He will let you know.

When it comes to critically examining media, he is constrained by the same, previously mentioned character flaws: he can't credibly comment on many specific things, and is unfortunately prone to offering blanket positive statements.

Weirdly, the only criticisms about which I feel seriously are the negative ones concerning things I enjoy. Diminish my work all you please, but come anywhere near criticising my taste, or the media I most cherish, and prepare to meet a furious, babbling, and unoriginal defender.

Since I can't proffer any coherent defences beyond my feelings, afforded in my mind a gravitas I seem to continuously find myself lacking in speech, I resort to positive criticism, the kind I have heard from others, and with which I generally agree.

Statements like 'I like the way that book was written' or 'I don't like the plot of this show' are rarely ones that would stand up to a simple 'Why?'

Instead, what I'm more likely to be heard saying is something like: 'I don't think that movie was badly lit, because a very reputable critic I like said it was reminiscent of Roger Deakins, who I'm sure is a fantastic cinematographer, because that same critic told me so.

Were he not such a hypocrite, my inner pedantic critic would be livid.

*

Not to sound my age, but there's a tweet I read a long time ago that I think about often, as it pertains to this discussion of criticism.

It said something along the lines of:

'A writer I respect once gave me the best advice of my career. When you get notes, listen to them. Smile. Nod. Disagree every once in a while. Then throw them away and make the book better. Just make it better, that's all you need to do – and you know how.'

I value those who know more than I do.

If these words ever see the light of day, it's because people far more experienced, intelligent, and patient than I made them better, and I agreed.

I'll listen to them.

I'll disagree every once in a while.

I'm way too big a pansy to throw away all their notes, but that doesn't mean I don't know my work. I am immensely grateful that the one aspect of my life from which I garner security is the ability to place a single word after another.

And another.

I wonder how many twenty-year-olds use the word 'pansy'.

The Two-Day Slump

I never put off till tomorrow what I can possibly
do the day after.

Oscar Wilde

A FRIEND ASKED me for advice about how to deal with bouts of procrastination.

Aware of my own struggles with procrastination, and either unaware of or unfazed by the fact that it's a problem I still regularly have to manage, my friend assured me it was my advice they wanted.

I suppose they recognised the fact they were addressing an expert in the field.

The first thought that entered my mind was the one I was most expecting, namely, that I'm the least qualified person out there to comment with a degree of optimism on the broad subject of procrastination.

I have spent half of my two decades on this mortal coil in some state of awareness of my fraught relationship with a healthy attitude to working. This is the majority of what takes up space in my long-term memory. I have had a decade of practice – a decade of experience that qualifies me not to opine on solving procrastination, but that has left me in just the position necessary to empathise with anyone else's struggles.

A significant early example of mine dates back to before my boarding school days, while living in Mumbai. I was no older than twelve, and had just heard about a major assignment for my favourite subject, Social Studies.

Around that time, when reaching the peak of my early

interest in Greek myths courtesy of the Rick Riordan *Percy Jackson* series, a class that provided a chance to study real battles and leaders in their historical context was right up my alley. It even maintained my interest as the curriculum was later focused in a more homeward direction. At this point I was able to channel my enthusiasm for those earlier topics within the subject, for a closer look at a slice of India's intriguing history.

I loved it, and I now marvel at the enthusiasm I felt to study a subject I would later treat with general indifference. But my interest was secured, and the assignment – designing a booth for our upcoming Social Studies class fair – would be the perfect occasion on which to focus and prove that abiding interest.

That didn't pan out, however.

It was sharing the responsibility of the design with a classmate. What our mutual passion for the subject enabled in lively and intriguing conversations, it lacked in any real sense of threat or initiative that is a constant need in my productive life. I am by no means blaming my classmate, who I recall sensing the fear before I did, as we started our better-late-than-never work on the booth.

The result could have generously been described as lacklustre.

While the other classmates had decked out their own spaces with drawings, diagrams, and elaborate dioramas, creating fantastic props with which to entertain their passers-by, visitors to our booth would have been greeted by a few bland pages of twelve-point text, pasted to a bare background of green construction paper.

Our showstopper was a bowlful of fact-laden flashcards presented on our assigned table. I cringe whenever reminded of the several times we attempted to impress the parents and faculty by fishing out a flashcard and reading verbatim.

Cringing aside, though, I actually enjoy reminiscing about this example.

In nascent stages, it demonstrates my chronic procrastination perfectly, but I am also able to look at it under a more forgiving lens. As I see it now, my classmate and I were working to the best of our abilities. Admittedly, our grades for this project were underwhelming, as we were simply not working under conditions that might see our abilities thrive.

I have since learned the significance of withholding judgement on myself for failing in situations in which I had no immediate ability, or desire to excel.

In addition to the fact-reading with my friend, that he and I compensated for with daunting enthusiasm, I recall us as having the booth at which visitors stayed the longest. We didn't have any slick artwork or models for them to admire. But we did spend effort engaging, and making conversation about the aspects of Indian history the facts referenced.

We were, after all, enamoured with the subject. And our interest was manifested less through visual medium, and more through the unbridled glee we needed little excuse to unleash.

My procrastination has since evolved.

Currently, I'm less likely to look favourably upon my misgivings, though if that is justified or likewise something to be remedied over time – I'm not sure. I was, though, able to extrapolate some advice for the friend who you may recall started this tangent.

It comes in two parts.

The first is a lesson which one could broadly have drawn from the tangent: it can be useful to have someone else. More often than not, other people can be guaranteed sources of distraction, but well-intentioned and focused, they can be contrived together to build a complete and perhaps perfect whole. Even if that almost-perfection is accidental.

As much as they can be distractions, people can also be reminders of the work to be done, especially if you're prescient enough to ask them to keep you on track.

The second piece of advice is rooted much more in my present, though it does still carry traces from my bare-booth example. It's to allow oneself to slump for a day, but ensure the next day achieves real productivity. I made an effort to draw attention to that lesson from my example, to look at yourself with a degree of forgiveness.

Don't work if you know you don't feel like it – that's largely fine – but don't cheapen it by making yourself feel bad for it at the same time. What that does is make you less likely to afford yourself such breaks in the future, while at the same time forcing you to wallow in unproductive ennui.

Enjoy the slump for a day.

But only the one day.

When you leave the slump, you'll still have some distance left to close.

And you'll close it even quicker.

Epistula

A letter always seemed to me like immortality because it is the mind alone without corporeal friend.

Emily Dickinson

DEAR SELF,

You're writing again – congratulations.

I don't know what it took for you to finally get back to doing that, but I'm certainly not complaining. Nor do I know the contents of this letter to come. We know each other, ourself, intimately. I know your faults. You know my worries. I know that it's really starting to bother you how much I've used the word 'know' in just this paragraph.

But you know I like the repetition, so indulge me.

We have never truly felt like a whole self. Or, rather, a *fullest* self. I'm sure there is something meta-textual about framing that fact within 'talking to myself', but rest assured that it is entirely unintentional.

Contrary to what we often think, our genius is usually stumbling onto a half-formed idea and wasting its potential.

But back to the subject of self; I honestly don't know how to define that within the context of us.

That feels disconcerting – why do we lack this supposed cohesion in identity that is touted as an immutable characteristic of the human condition?

I know what you are, what I am. We are a collection of feelings, wisps of emotion that blow through our soul and confuse us, excite us, frighten us, and encourage us. We fleet and are fleeted through the chaos of consciousness. That last sentence sounded good. We are at the mercy of ourselves –

beholden to a power that is out of our grasp.

Why are you writing this now? We love to write, yes, but that's never been a factor motivating enough to be translated into the present continuous.

Instead, you love to idealise it:

Oh, I'm such a good writer.

My erudition is clear, my vocabulary is complex.

When I write I feel a fragment of that power.

And there it goes.

That split second of control exists to create for us a gossamer thread of connection, an addiction – there but barely strong enough to be acted on. It's far easier an alternative to sit there and know that you can write well, content in the fact that doing so brings joy.

There was the word again – *know*.

That's our real addiction.

When I write, I am in my element as much as that is possible, because I'm making sense of fleeting sentiments bared by my soul, and wisps of fading and transient notions.

It is the only space in which I feel my own capacity to turn an 'I think' into an 'I know'. What little we know about ourselves and each other comes from this. And whatever is trapped in the filter, that which we are unable to convey in a series of words we like, is lost to us.

The truth is made subjective in us, but it is made.

Dear Other,

You're right.

And oh – look how happy that's made you!

Yes, we're right, but only because it takes more effort than it appears worth to be anything else. The state of our knowledge is small and malleable, and of little real-world import, I think. So, in life, you hide behind ambivalence, and well-intentioned ignorance.

You feel underqualified – and perhaps you are – to opine on anything of any actual significance, and cling instead to the sanctity of trivial facts and their logic – willing to die on a molehill, for mountains require too much new perspective.

We have enough perspective of our own, don't we? In books we enjoy we have discovered facts that haven't been questioned, but don't appear to be doing anyone any harm.

Is *that* why you enjoy writing?

I imagine it is.

Here, odd word choice and unnecessary amounts of consecutive clauses feel less out of place. In this snug world of my design, those trivialities we clasp so tight against our chest, defended with unneeded gusto, can be placed on a more substantial stage.

With words, I might as well be an ancient Roman orator having a constant existential crisis. Aside from my evident and too-rarely judged ego, that statement seeks to convey a sense of power within this medium, one that is focused directly inwards.

It walks the halls of my mind, finding concealed staircases I didn't realise existed, unlocking timeworn and rusted gates. Neither of us knows what this random internal exploration will yield. The answer, unfortunately, has so far had the tendency of being an uncomfortable truth or an incomplete whole – what will forever remain no more than a fragment.

It can be comforting, then, to take solace in the delicious fact that I know only a fraction of what I'm going to know. However much I think I know and however much I actually do exist at the top of a graph. But the x-axis ends in today, and observed too closely, one might think that the 'final' point – the total amount I know – remains unmoving. Context alone can prove that the axes are still growing and that precious amount is only greater still.

Writing is one of the only things that falls in the precious middle of our least favourite Venn diagram. The circle on the left is labelled 'things we like doing', and 'things that are at least a little productive' sits to its right. It carries with it the added bonus of allowing me to act as my own unqualified therapist, which in lieu of any actionable progress, leaves me with an unearned sense of accomplishment, and a series of inconclusive answers.

My words weren't as pretty as yours.

We sourced them from the same well, but you dressed them up more handsomely, tried to make something respectable of something we scarcely understand. There are occasions and talents, and inclinations for pretty words that don't always present themselves, that can make this venture we both enjoy so much maddeningly inconsistent.

I may be regressing, or making the wrong mistakes, but as long as I follow your guidance and try to make mistakes in the right direction... who knows?

I never do.

Dangerous Motivations

Everywhere is walking distance if you have the time.

Paul Valéry

You HAVE READ of my procrastination.

But another reason I don't write as much as I'd like to is a lack of motivation.

Even in the times when I have felt it, the extra effort it calls for compared with my default preoccupation with watching a movie or a show, makes it a challenge to start.

Despite this, there are times at which I am overcome with a motivation and desire to embark on something categorically productive. The catch, though, is that I have never followed through in such instances. I spend a lot of time wishing I didn't feel that overwhelming sense of initiative at all.

For a little while I'm going to exchange the thesis for some context.

Allow me to set the scene.

Over the past two years, I have found great comfort in going on hours-long walks in and to places I know. The routes are unchanging, identical to those I took on whatever occasion saw me take them for the first time – be it errand, curiosity, or boredom.

I can recall about a dozen of them now, in three separate countries. I adore finding them by chance, organically, whenever I've begun to settle into a new city. I derive a sense of security in having the same route to follow.

You see, I'm a creature of habit.

The times at which I am keen to set out with no preprogrammed destination, prepared and eager to get lost and find myself, are rare.

Aside from the actual activity contained therein, these walks are made interesting by one of two accompaniments, although more usually a combination of both.

The first is my unceasing, my infinite internal monologue, to which I will return in a moment.

The second is whatever aural media I happen to be in the mood for – whether it be a podcast, an audiobook, or, more often than not, a favourite shuffled playlist. Each of them works to prompt a different part of the internal monologue, in different ways.

In that respect, audiobooks are the most restrictive, but are a medium I enjoy regardless of that fact. A characteristic of their consumption I've come to appreciate is the ability to have a tangential stream of thought in the middle of a sentence, while still grasping enough of what occurred during my lapse of attention to render rewinding unnecessary.

Music, on the other hand, is far more valuable as a source of background vibrations. I am able to take pleasure in the awareness that I enjoy the song, while letting my mind wander as I tread a path trodden countless times before.

When music is the chosen source of entertainment, an unregulated and unstructured stream of motivation and inspiration tends to present itself, and more out of happenstance than any train of thought.

Podcasts facilitate the most nuanced reactions, and provide mental rabbit holes into which I find myself diving deep. While a certain amount of that can be reasonably chalked up to the breadth of podcasts that I have on regular rotation, my favourites can be distilled into the following genres of comedy, news, comedic news, stories and folklore, films, media discussions, and the classic category of people I enjoy listening to, engaged in a conversation with another.

A commonality between them that I've been able to extrapolate is that they all involve these disembodied voices talking with infectious enthusiasm about what they live and love to do.

That, or the same message conveyed through my enjoyment of their work.

The *Myths and Legends* podcast is one of my favourite examples of this.

It consists of a husband-and-wife team uncovering lesser-known myths and well-known legends with noteworthy origins, and breathing new life into them through contemporary storytelling techniques.

Equally, I adore listening to filmmakers waxing lyrical about why they are so enamoured with their craft, the films that made them, and how they hope their own work will inspire others.

Appreciating the hard work but undeniable skill of such creators is magical.

So, now, motivation rears its ugly head. In those moments of pure and unbridled appreciation, I become consumed with a concentrated desire to follow my own dreams, to create my own art.

Why this is an issue requires, unfortunately, a bit more context.

Most of the time, I take these walks at night.

They rarely occur when there is any sunlight at all. The one thing I have in common with Taylor Swift is that whenever I am in a routine which allows for such nocturnal strolls, it creates a period of time in which I have let, as she puts it, 'midnights become my afternoons'.

But starting any productive effort that late at night, even knowing the preceding fact to be true, is unprecedented and improbable. My body is not a natural habitat for motivation, so, once sighted, it tends to have an expected lifespan of no more than thirty minutes.

So, the following is the situation I find myself in on these walks.

It's late.

Most cinemas have let out their last patrons and locked their doors, and I've invariably just grabbed dinner at a fast-food joint. I pick from one of my pre-loaded routes and set off, with a podcast episode about Billy Wilder's *The Apartment* encompassing me through my noise-cancelling headphones.

A mile or two in, paying attention to the episode while simultaneously thinking about other media I've consumed on different days at that exact spot, one of the voices says something – a quote or a sentiment expressed – to which I feel a profound connection. I find the journey of others towards meaning relatable, as it itself contributes a little to my own sense of meaning.

In the moment, such motivation is a swelling and warming joy.

But, as things stand, it's nothing more than accidental,

and so of little *actionable* use to me right now.

Despite that, and my lukewarm reaction to it at the start of this piece, I value this incidental motivation whenever it arises – if only for its capacity to generate a memory for myself of a time in which creating something was my truest desire.

For now, though, I'm content to outsource it.

Final Status Pending

A picture held us captive. And we could not get outside it, for it lay in our language and language seemed to repeat it to us inexorably.

Ludwig Wittgenstein

IT IS A BRIGHT, warm day in Venice.

The late afternoon sun touches my neck and my skin, and it feels like I'm shining, like my insides are glowing. I am on my first day of a month-long trip through Italy with two close friends. I'd travelled before, and spent plenty of time that felt my own, but where I was in that moment in Venice felt like a perfect marriage of the two.

As much soul-searching and self-improvement as I find in my own words, I learn most about myself when in the company of my friends. There's plenty about myself to be found in the company of those I dislike, but that seems like a less constructive avenue along which to venture. The revelations – if I can get away with calling them that – which present themselves while in the company of friends come in good and bad flavours.

Interestingly, it is only when I am away from friends for long stretches of time that I allow myself to wallow in such revelations. The simple pleasure of enjoying a moment with others is that it can only really be savoured from within. The most I can do from the outside is appreciate it, an appreciation that too often curdles into pining.

Those weeks in Italy now seem to me to exist in that indeterminable limbo between the sentiments 'gosh, that was a while ago', and 'it feels like it was just last week'. And I'm glad. That unique blend offers the benefit of looking back *sans* rose-tinted lenses, yet with feelings fresh enough to fondly recall.

I can recollect, for example, the jokes created in and only for that time.

And I remember falling sick in Rome and missing out on the Vatican.

There was the triumphant sense of dropping down the heavy duffel bag and sinking into my hostel bed after the long trek from the station – through a city we would begin to explore just minutes later. And the feeling of having my social batteries drained, and the new kind of exhaustion it brought. I remember the sheer volume of food we devoured in those four weeks.

That I could even find myself on an adventure like this was something which would have seemed far-fetched until then. My life in school and out of it were two different worlds – two spheres that only had me in common. And my friends only existed in that school sphere.

I had spent the majority of time around my friends there, and yet any events of note were skewed towards my out-of-school life, away from my friends. Italy, then, seemed to be an overdue and proper convergence of those spheres.

This came to a head during my first stab at university, in which the non-school life felt more like my own. It was lacking in other social connections which, until that point, it seemed like I'd been denied. My mood was one of frustration, closeness developed too late to provide comfort when it felt like I really needed it.

The irritation was tied to something else – a fact I have

mulled over and debated internally ad nauseam, towards an unsatisfying conclusion. Even if I could go back in time, or rather, start anew – knowing what I know now – I have little confidence in my ability to make meaningful changes in my social life.

That can be broken down into two parts.

The first is the relationship between nature and nurture – the answer to which I sense lies somewhere in the gradient between them.

In my case, sociability struggles are either late-onset nature, or delayed-reaction nurture. I've carried growing versions of such struggles since approximately age ten – I suppose it was the first time I ever had to *think about* making friends.

The second part refers to the awareness I have of my deficiencies in socialising, which has done nothing to actually help. I know that life would have been a hell of a lot more pleasant if I had branched out and talked to people more upon first joining boarding school. Knowing doesn't change the fact that I didn't, and don't even know that I could.

It's an issue that I still have next to no idea about how to behave in a setting like that. Because this is not something most people have to think about, I don't think.

Being in a social setting with my friends is utter bliss, because I don't have to listen as much to my deafening internal monologue.

Being in a social setting with strangers, or people with whom I am not comfortable, is my idea of hell, complete with that damned internal monologue, refusing to shut up.

Italy was the former, and honestly far better than I could

ever have imagined.

I had been finishing up a year in which everything I thought I knew, everything I expected to happen had fallen apart, and all I really needed were friends beside me, to help me pick up the pieces.

In a favourite TV show of mine, *The Newsroom*, about a team of altruistic, painfully mortal cable news journalists, there's a line that comforts me. Recognising his position as a role model and as a shield for his staff, the anchor allays a colleague's worries by telling her that 'if there's any fallout, [he'll] be standing right next to her and in front. [He'll] always be standing right next to her and in front'.

That is exactly the kind of simple assurance I feel with my close friends, and crave when I'm without them. They shield me and guide me as I stumble forwards, convincing me I'm not as much of a basket case as I think I am.

And I like to think that in my own way, I'm there to offer them a fraction of the support they give me. I'm in a good place, now. Or better, at least.

That's got to count for something.

I hope it does one day.

Pro Concession

So far, about morals, I know only that what is moral is what you feel good after and what is immoral is what you feel bad after.

Ernest Hemingway, *Death in the Afternoon*

Cold air. Colder water.

Like fingers and slamming car doors, being at the intersection of those two things is a less than pleasant experience. Made worse still, as is the case in this convergence of frigid elements, by being a result of poor, yet characteristically consistent, decision-making.

He was fortunate to have attended a school with excellent sports facilities. He was foolish enough, however, to have *repeatedly* pursued an elusive athletic career in rowing or kayaking, while being presented with clear indications from his peers that doing as much was inadvisable.

Welcome to court.

I'll be playing the roles of prosecution, defence, judge, and jury, in this not-at-all one-sided discussion that will allow me to rummage through thoughts, and dissect how defensible they are, ignoring the most apparent error in judgement currently visible: that this sentence is easily three times longer than it needs to be. This is surely an apt moment to mention that my grasp of the processes and intricacies of law comes from misremembered snippets of legal dramas on television.

Court is in session.

Bangs gavel

We, the defence, recognise the appeals to idiocy that the prosecution made in the opening paragraph to this piece

– their statement. We recognise them as baseless, and seek only to emphasise the fault in perspective.

That false equivalency about the fingers in the car door notwithstanding – what the fine members of the jury ought to take into consideration are the good qualities Timur has gleaned as a result of this experience. He is a little more capable of handling cold weather. He spent at least some of that time breathless on the water, yes, but in the company of people who would become casual acquaintances.

Moreover, his commitment to this water-sport challenge speaks to his dedication, to his fitness-oriented mind, and to the school spirit. We maintain that the whole experience was character-building, and something of which to be proud.

We, the jury, find this thought to be... bad. Your Honour?

Thank you, foreperson, and if I may proffer my own opinion, I agree wholeheartedly. I mean, the boy came dead last in the two competitive kayaking races he was asked to participate in – I hardly think that contributed much to an overall positive experience. Also, I hold disdain for the term 'character-building'. It always seems like someone on the ropes, scrambling for a defence.

Alright, let's see what we have next on the docket.

Ah of course, *The Mind vs. University, The First Time* Prosecution, the floor is yours.

Thank you, Your Honour.

This seems like an open-and-shut case if ever there was one. I mean, is he seriously suggesting his decision to attend university in a city he barely knew, for a course he chose with little forethought, that saw him live for six months in an environment in which he rarely engaged with anyone – *was good?*!

Despite living four minutes' walk away from campus, he had to attend his 8 a.m. lectures online. He learned virtually nothing, made no meaningful connections, and spent his Christmas that year alone, his only companions a handful of shows he'd already seen and two large Domino's pepperoni pizzas. In what possible way could any of that be construed as a positive experience?

The defence thanks the prosecution for their rhetorical question and we would be glad to answer it. The beauty in this decision Timur made, and the facts that make up for the adverse aspects we do not deny, concern two simple truths.

The first is that those negative elements were significant, but not a majority. That decision enabled the first sense of independence he had ever encountered, and gave Timur a glimpse of himself in a facsimile of the real world.

He became more comfortable in his own company.

He learned things about himself within the university experience – including the various reasons that the kind of teaching he was encountering was not conducive to his academic learning.

He learned that Christmas is just another day, and that Domino's pizza is delicious. Actually, it's even more so when paired with a beloved sitcom – after all, people just seem funnier and more beautiful when viewed through the lens of TV.

The second of those two truths is just as crucial: it was the only way to get to where he is now, where he is mostly happy to be.

We, the jury, find this thought to be... good. Judge Timur?

Thank you, yes. As heart-warming a defence as I've ever heard. Which brings us to our final case for this evening. If I'm not mistaken, it is *The Mind vs. Deserved Confidence*. Prosecution?

We take this third case the most seriously. To remind the jury, the thought currently on trial is the one summoned from the depths of Timur's mind, when he, in the company of a friend, thought: *I hate that they're more confident than me, because I feel like I deserve to be the confident one.*

There's a lot to unpack there. None of it looks good.

Being so jealous, so hateful, to wish the confidence of a friend was their own? For shame. Allow me to point out, as well, the train of thought that enabled this particular notion to arise.

Timur thought himself better looking than his friend, and smarter, too. The only (unnecessary) reaction to that was the one begrudging his friend for possessing a quality he himself lacked. He felt vain, insecure, prideful, and that manifested into a singularly cruel thought.

The prosecution rests.

It was wrong. He knows it was wrong. The defence rests.

We, the jury, find this thought to be... actually, we couldn't decide between good and bad for this one. That means you have to pick, right, Your Honour?

Uh... *checks notes*... yes? Sure. Yes.

Well, I am disappointed, but admittedly unsurprised at this outcome. I like when there's a straight good or bad, a right or wrong – when one side just made more sense.

But they both did.

Timur was undoubtedly in the wrong for thinking what he did, but at least had the decency to recognise it as wrong. Maybe decency is the wrong word.

Does he feel shame? I imagine so – I see no other reason for him to have created this silly little literary law house.

To put himself on trial in front of his readers – perhaps.

To put himself on trial in front of *himself* – yes, I imagine so.

No juror, real or invented, scares him more than *himself*. That shame the prosecutor called for, I get the feeling that it has gotten to him already. Mostly for the thought, but probably at least in part for talking about himself in the third person for as long as he has. For now, I suppose knowing he was wrong – and will likely continue to be – will have to do.

Case closed.

Court is adjourned.

Demonstratum

Trivia is a fact without a home.

Don Rittner

Now FOR AN intermission – well, an intermission of sorts.

I, of all people, know how draining it can be to spend too much time in the company of my thoughts. So, before I inflict more of myself upon you, I'd like to tell you a story.

Yes, I'd *like* to tell you a story, but I have tried and tried and found that I have none to tell. The best one I can summon is a long, ham-fisted metaphor.

So, apologies, but it'll have to do.

This particular adventure pertains to the treasured occasions on which I competed in inter-house general knowledge competitions at school. The rules were simple, and modelled on the popular English quiz show *University Challenge*.

Two teams of four would face off against each other, with each team having a member nominated as captain. The first question of each round was open to anyone – we all had buzzers, and could chime in with an answer, although we weren't allowed to confer with our teammates. The team with the winning answer would be awarded three follow-up questions.

Before I explain the other rules – as is unnecessary to this story but nonetheless important to me that I do – I want to stress how much I valued taking part in these annual competitions.

There were a dozen other inter-house events throughout

the year for which students could represent their house. And, as much as I dislike sports, what has been evident all my life is how little the abstract concept of sports cared for me. We keep a wary distance from each other.

House Challenge, then, this battle of useless general knowledge, was the one field in which I could serve as a proud ambassador of my house.

If you got the buzzer question right, the three questions were your team's opportunity to put some distance between yourselves and your opponents. The three follow-ups would be related to each other in some obvious or, as was more common, a more esoteric way – one that made answering the questions a potentially solvable problem if you didn't already know the answer.

Conferring was permitted, but only the team captain could voice the team's answer, unless they nominated one of their teammates in the interest of speed or pronunciation. Games only lasted twenty minutes.

Questions answered incorrectly would be passed to the opposing team, as a chance for them to win the ten points each correct answer afforded. A correctly answered buzzer question followed by three correct follow-ups was worth an extra ten.

We never lost a game.

Okay, *fine*, we did lose a few of the inter-school games, but I maintain that those were rigged against us.

During four out of five of my years at the school, though, I competed in at least three games a year, and never lost a House Challenge game.

I don't remember most of the questions. Of those I do, though, very few of them are the ones I got right.

The ones I got wrong have stuck with me.

What is the first property on a Monopoly board?

What is the word used to describe a Roman government run by three men?

Who looked out 'on the Feast of Stephen'?

The feeling of unknowing wasn't then the one I am now used to – it wasn't shame.

No, it was a small anger, a subdued tension within me. I desperately wanted to know the correct answer, and I wanted to know it forever. Then there were the reactions of others, of the history teachers who obviously knew the years when ancient events started and ended, and the friend of mine who said he could name every single property on the Monopoly board.

Those bothered me.

But not because they underscored my failures, but because they diminished my successes. I got those questions wrong, yes, *but I got so many others right – ones that you probably wouldn't have.*

Remember those depths.

When I said a little earlier that the questions I remember are the ones I got wrong, I hinted to and breezed past a subset, i.e. the questions I answered correctly.

In my penultimate year at school, during House Challenge season, there was one game in which I was not allowed to play. A boy in my house, in the year above, had never played a game and wanted to take this opportunity to do so. In the interest of fairness and team spirit, I was asked to bow out for the quarter-final.

But I still went to watch it. It was infuriating.

My house emerged narrowly as the victors of that game. Listening to the questions the team – 'we' – got wrong frustrated and angered me to a dangerously visible extent. Part of that anger lay in the fact that it was possible we wouldn't make it to the final.

Yet more derived from the point that, despite knowing the answers to most of the questions they got wrong, I was not showered with the adulation I craved.

Who ran the first sub-four-minute mile?

In the television show, who 'won' Game of Thrones?

Who was the Greek goddess of the hunt?

Considering it since, it has become clear to me how those experiences were demonstrations of the relationship I have with information.

I regard facts, and the telling of them, as party tricks.

Poor party tricks, perhaps, but no more than ways in which I can show off. A sorry substitute for skill. I wanted to know these things – like I now know about Old Kent Road, triumvirates, and King Wenceslaus – but I wanted to bask in the credit.

Now, I have to confess that I lied to you at the start.

I said I had a story to tell, and that wasn't quite true. We are all incomplete collections of experiences – experiences which are occasionally insightful, but more often they are condemned to live and die in their lack of individual context.

And that's an unsolvable problem.

I also said that I had a metaphor, and that wasn't exactly true, either. Life is not a metaphor for itself. Things and experiences don't have to (and usually don't) mean anything more substantive, anything more than what appears right there on the surface, skin-deep.

Truthfully, I didn't, and still don't, know what I had.

When I sit down and squander those distracted hours in front of a computer screen mining myself for words, two particular thoughts tend to take centre stage in my mind.

Firstly, I think too much.

And secondly, I don't think enough.

So much of the 'me' others see, I find, is the me that I am attempting to convince you actually exists. I choose the light you see me in. That extends to my perceived intellect, and to how interesting I believe I am; the long-winded example above suggests as much. Increasingly, more of that me has devolved into trying to convince my own mind of these same truths.

As I see it, my only job is to find that inner convincer, and beat the living daylights out of him.

He's done enough damage to the perceptions others hold of me.

He's done enough damage to me.

Trivial

If you are losing your leisure, look out!
– It may be you are losing your soul.

Virginia Woolf

I AM KING of the Trivial.

It's a title emblematic of a relationship that's taken me a good long while to get used to – between being *good at something*, and being good enough at something.

I'm still only just getting used to it.

As is the case with most of my self-diagnosed behaviour and personality.

Being used to it reflects a degree of comfort I ought to accept.

That is, once one takes into account how many other frayed strands of my being never come close to being solved, only resolved to being ignored lest they give me an ulcer.

I know four card tricks.

I can juggle three balls for an average of thirty seconds.

I can solve a Rubik's cube in under a minute.

And I can name the capital of every country in the world.

We'll get to the memory stuff later, but it's something else I can use to pad out this list. So, what does this all add up to? Well, aside from sounding like the CV of a particularly enterprising eight-year-old, they are the little things I do to stave off productivity, while at the same time achieving a modest sense of accomplishment.

I've seen a graph that purports to chart the rate of the progress of learning a new skill. It's a steep line upwards, followed by a plateau, and another less steep line which ends in mastery – mastery being a slow flattening of the curve, as opposed to another abrupt plateau.

In most cases, I am content to set my expectations at the plateau, the stage at which one gains a reasonable degree of proficiency at the skill, but before extra commitment is required for a real attempt at mastery.

There are people out there who can solve Rubik's cubes in under ten seconds; people who can juggle half a dozen balls while making cool patterns in the air; people who have devoted their lives to performing a handful of card tricks faultlessly.

They are not me, and I am more than happy to make that distinction.

In all my facets of work, I am far more concerned with making it *appear* as though I've put in time and effort than actually putting in the time and effort.

Coming to terms with that point made it easier to arrive at the conclusion that I don't go to these 'lengths' out of any dedication to personal enrichment. Rather, my motivation comes from the misguided hope that such 'achievements' raise the opinions that others hold of me.

Thankfully, I'm moving away from that as motivation.

Not only is it personally unfulfilling, but it is extremely ineffective. I imagine some of you are wondering what kinds of people would be impressed by my ability to perform a mediocre card vanish. Believe me, I'm still reeling from the fact that I didn't wonder that from the start. This whole line of thinking notwithstanding, I'm not going to quit on my pursuit of the trivial.

Instead, I'm finding different reasons to take pride in it.

The Rubik's cube, for example, has been upgraded from lacklustre party trick to a fidget device used to keep my hands busy whenever I'm nervous.

Then there's the memory stuff I mentioned earlier. In this case, it's completely unrelated to my experiential memory, focusing more on what I've learned by rote. This is what began my personal appreciation for the trivial. It started when I learned the 'To be or not to be' and 'Tomorrow and tomorrow and tomorrow' soliloquies.

It takes at least two minutes to rattle off the former with appropriate gusto, but it soon became apparent that attempting to hold someone's attention for that long was asking a bit too much and, frankly, counterproductive.

So, I found another reason to do it.

In the time I spent reading and rereading Percy Bysshe Shelley, Philip Larkin, and William Ernest Henley, my relationship with poetry as a medium intensified, and my appreciation for the subtle and overt beauty they all contained only grew deeper.

I came to find and discern my own meaning in my meetings with 'a traveller from an antique land', 'fools in old-style hats and coats' and 'the menace of the years'[1]. They taught me that words can be used in much more compelling and emotionally resonant ways than the literal, although that is a lesson I am continuing to take in.

---

[1] From Shelley's *Ozymandias*, Larkin's *This Be The Verse*, and Henley's *Invictus*, respectively.

Rote memorisation is a perfect example of where things currently stand for my continued passion for the trivial: set goals. Some are easier than others, but it has so far served me well to seek the same checkpoints of success in less binary tasks.

Can I disappear a card well enough to impress my friends or make them laugh?

Great.

Can I juggle for thirty seconds straight?

Good enough for me.

Learning the capital cities of every country came with the easiest measure of success, and with the side effect of learning that certain countries I'd never heard of exist. When I find myself in an early stage of a trivial pursuit, I make sure to include a step that has me decide what I am trying to get out of this – namely, how this pursuit will end.

If there's one thing I want to make sure any new endeavour in this space avoids, it's making me feel bad – or worse, guilty – about failure. No one likes failing at something important, but failing at something trivial can be a completely different, more bitter kind of demoralising.

Given my propensity for despondency, the solution I've had to bodge together to ensure as little of that disappointment as possible seeps into my head is, as this sentence suggests, in the scale of it all.

The key is volume.

Why beat myself up about not continuing to try to cultivate the skills required to memorise the order of a shuffled deck of cards, when I could supercharge my other 'skill' of solving a Rubik's cube by learning to do it blindfolded? I never did learn how, but I had already started my next venture before feeling bad about that one had even occurred to me. It is its own kind of boundary-setting, one that helps me optimise the relationship between getting the most out of an idle hobby while still feeling pleased about myself.

Sure, it would be really cool if I could speak ten languages with fluency, but I can make idle conversation in at least four, which is far better than nothing. It's come to the point that I consider the graph I mentioned earlier existing as two separate wholes.

The first graph comprises a steep line that takes someone from no experience to a state of relative comfort. In most of my cases, that constitutes a complete unit. A completely separate endeavour, which I am welcome to take of my own volition, is what the second graph represents, a concerted effort to take what is no more than a basic skill, and devote the time and work to achieve real proficiency.

Setting low standards for oneself can be an impressive source of self-worth.

Twenty-Hood

A brilliant ball, gay with light romance laughter, wears through its own silks and satins to show the bare framework of a man-made thing – oh, that eternal hand! – a play, most tragic and most divine, becomes merely a succession of speeches, sweated over by the eternal plagiarist in the clammy hours and acted by men subject to cramps, cowardice, and manly sentiment.

F. Scott Fitzgerald, *The Beautiful and Damned*

By the time any sort of audience sees this book, what they are reading will most likely have changed a great deal.

Or not – I have no idea.

At the time of writing this, I am nineteen years old, and I find it absolutely baffling that I am not yet in my twenties. I mean, it feels as though I already am.

Or, at least, that I ought to be.

Any time I hear reference to someone's twenties – if it was something they did, somewhere they went or some *whatever* they *whatevered* – I can relate. Not to the content of their experiences – in fact, that's usually the subject of my desire or envy. Hope, if you're feeling charitable.

Instead, the common ground I mistakenly sense derives from the fact that I feel like I'm at the same stage of my life as the one they are describing.

I am in my twenties.

Although, of course, I am not.

But why do I have to routinely remind myself of it?

What does it say about me, and what does it say about the world that I've lived in that made me believe it?

There is no one answer, I think.

The point at which one may begin is by examining the different ways people visualise time – time as it pertains to people and their individual environments. It's that latter part that I find most interesting, because it speaks to the ways in which our minds reflect our existence as a whole.

A very surface-level example of this would be how, whenever I think of a calendar, the image conjured in my mind's eye is the same colour scheme as a calendar that hung on the wall of my classroom when I was six years old.

But that's not my point.

My point is that a minute is not a minute and time is not time. It's not a new idea by any means, but on the scale of seconds as well as years, our metrics can feel like estimates at best. Interchangeable, even. I've lived minutes that felt like hours and weeks that felt like a handful of seconds. And I'm not even twenty yet.

At this point, it almost seems as though I am making a case for my being twenty on account of feeling it. After all, the measurements we ascribe to time, and the societal boundaries we fill in after the fact, are by no means set in stone.

But being in one's twenties isn't a societal boundary in the same way turning eighteen gives you the right to vote. I have yet to experience it, but by all accounts, the clock striking midnight on one's twentieth birthday doesn't suddenly make you privy to never-before-considered categories of thought, nor is it like reaching a checkpoint in a video game.

It's a day like any other.

That's why I'm not trying to say that I'm already twenty. That would be an inane statement to make, I know, but on more than just a factual basis.

For starters, I don't feel *completely* twenty, and the reasons for the falter in that feeling are exactly why I'm not making that argument.

I have spent my entire media-consuming life consuming media that's had something to say about going through your twenties. Within them, it's treated like a given, as though these are experiences we can all expect to enjoy, and laugh and suffer through. An unfortunate sense of expectation has developed within me. Being under twenty, however, I know that I am in the minority of their viewership, and so, therefore, is my perspective – or lack of one.

Of course, though, that hasn't stopped me from enjoying this media. *How I Met Your Mother*, my favourite sitcom, is a show I've adored since before I understood it. Nowadays, it's a show I continue to delight in, despite not being able to fully relate to it. This has had me wondering about the intention of its writers. I am younger than the audience for which it was originally written.

Given this, it doesn't feel like a logical leap to assume that my enjoyment of it is stifled by or, at the very least, different as a result of my inability to relate.

I have no stories, no life experiences to map onto the antics of a group of friends going through their late twenties in New York City. As with many things in life, I wish these sets of experience were a quantifiable object on which I could rely, and use almost as a personal guide. Rather like a progress bar that, once filled, would tell me that I've reached the sufficient level of relevant experience to get the absolute most meaning out of it.

The opposite of this fact has presented itself in the media I have found relatable. Except in those cases, it's never been a matter of direct comparison of lived experience, but rather being able to identify and understand mental states and trains and patterns of thought.

Charlie Chaplin once said that the difference between comedy and drama is distance. Sally Rooney's *Normal People* is a book I related to greatly when I first read it. In it, the audience is treated to a close and intimate look into the lives of two characters – Connell and Marianne – as their lives take them from school to university.

Their relationship has its moments of bliss and pathos, and fits comfortably in its genre. Relating too much to *How I Met Your Mother's* protagonist, Ted, would feel strange in comparison. It would seem out of place for the show to be constantly zooming in and out of comedy and drama, weighed down by the gravity with which I regard my own experiences. I don't relate to *How I Met Your Mother*. Considering it, I am content for that to be true forever – unless, that is, I find a personal layer that runs the risk of misappropriating the meaning.

I've gone on enough about the relationship between my idea of one's twenties and the pop culture I consume – at least for now. So, it's as good a time as any to share something of what I had in mind for that time, in both hopeful and realistic expectation.

First of all, I imagined everything would go according to plan.

Not to say that I had much of a plan at all (nor that I have one now, really), but in a way, it meant that I genuinely anticipated my expectations coming to pass. Big surprise, I know, though it seemed reasonable enough to be able to predict with my unspecific accuracy roughly what stage of life I'd been in a year or two down the line.

Nowadays, that timeline lands me square in my early twenties, and my expectations persist, but with an additional complication. This weird gap, between becoming an adult in the eyes of others and entering my twenties was proving, for me at least, rather important.

The feeling of it all counted for much more than I was expecting, and in looking for it in the future, and other unreliable places, it demonstrated the lesson I'm still trying to learn:

I can't rely on or trust such expectations, nor can I always trust myself.

I can firmly trace the expectations to media that I've consumed (yes, I'm back to talking about pop culture, and no, that tangent didn't last long). I admit it – almost none of my ideas are original. And, in this instance, there were precious few other places I could have turned to for a seemingly accurate representation of my future.

While I only came to this conclusion in writing this and forcing these notions into coherence, it must have occurred to me that there was nobody in my life with whom I could relate enough to form a basis for credible expectations. Angst and self-consciousness, though shared by my peers, were the point at which the similarities ended. Even still, they were fit to represent no more than the present, and neurological and social perspectives different to my own.

So, I settled for the next best thing: the aspirational sheen of life that is the sitcom status quo.

In lieu of a hyper-specific person I could relate to, my brain instead chose to extract a comfort of delusion and ersatz connection from fictional characters.

Again, I tender as an example *How I Met Your Mother*, as I know it so awkwardly well.

Let's consider what was in the picture of the reality it presented.

The protagonist, Ted Mosby, lives in New York City with his best friend and college roommate, Marshall Erikson.

Right away, I find that personally implausible, even if it's just the first sentence of a standard and inoffensive premise. I could go on, elaborating about the characters' friends, Barney and Robin, and Marshall's partner Lily, and the antics they get up to across the course of the show's nine seasons. But at least part of my conceptualisation of being in one's twenties stems from the fact that I have grown to idealise and expect those bar-room antics.

I'm not even focusing exclusively on the more *out there* plot points of the show, like licking the Liberty Bell, or designing a skyscraper, or starting an all-lawyer funk band, but the simple things like having a group of friends as close as they are and seeing them on a regular basis seem like admirable things to expect. This is why, except on occasions such as this, I try to avoid deconstructing the beautiful lie, because believing in it is half the fun.

Another thing... the Covid quarantine affected this perception of my twenty-hood.

The requiem for the boarding school student should be played on the world's smallest violin, yet there are bound to be at least minor complications to an event that takes someone who lives with and spends the majority of their time in the company of their friends, and puts them in a situation that deprives them of both.

I've spent the past six or so years of my life growing up (a process that is still very much ongoing), and about a third of that time was spent doing it on my own, while wishing my friends and I hadn't grown up in different directions.

Without even a semblance of a foundation, it became harder and harder for me to even form the expectations I wanted.

There's an interesting quirk, here, in the way people perceive time.

During the Covid lockdowns, plenty of material was published that said something to the effect of 'with a lack of regular, novel stimuli, individual memory retention decreases, our short-term memories blend with those further in the past than is the norm, and the overall result is that time can feel as though it is passing at an accelerated or abbreviated rate'.

Simply put, when fewer new things happen to us, less time appears to have passed.

My supposedly valuable youth, then, had become a commodity of which I could never take full advantage; I was eighteen before I had even become used to telling people I was seventeen. Twenty started to feel less like an expected inevitability, and more like a rapidly accelerating hurdle.

There are, of course, no real expectations placed on a twenty-year-old, at least not that I have experienced. Twenty isn't even what weighs on my mind, that word would be the similar sounding but vastly different 'twenties'. And not everyone has this fascination – obsession – with that decade of life.

I've asked others my age, and this cocktail of anticipation and ignorance is apparently my own. Barriers of age are as arbitrary as those dividing generations. Those barriers, though, particularly on the generational side of the discussion, can infect one's identity in subtle yet undeniable ways.

When encountering a video or post online that says something about the 'generation' to which I belong – 'Gen Z' – I unconsciously slip into an in-group, a hive mindset, before reacting.

Positive comments about this generation deliver me a great and unearned pride, while criticism of any kind awakens a defensiveness that I couldn't support with logic or tact. In that same vein, the arbitrary identity I feel is ascribed to someone in their twenties is one, I confess, I don't understand at all.

Something I expect to form a decent part of my identity is just missing. I hate how common that is for me.

Unfortunately, I don't see that gap being filled in by small parts of a cooler me to come. Rather, I see a blank space that will remain a vacuum, and which will contribute even more to the ever-present feeling of insecurity about who I am, who I *think* I am.

Parts of this mess aren't as bad as they seem to me much of the time. Indeed, parts almost make me hopeful.

Here's a silly example of the former:

I have spent the past two years entrenching myself in

the world of film and television. Critics whose opinions I respect, and whose recommendations I wish to honour, seem to have a collective familiarity, impossibly aware of every new masterpiece that is released.

Catching up, for whatever degree of unrealistic a goal it may be, is something I've been trying to do in this time, admonishing myself for time spent failing to engage with this art.

For crying out loud, I only watched the Hollywood classic *Casablanca* for the first time two years ago, despite the fact that I lived in the eponymous city for the first decade of my life.

The fact that I have not seen the collected works of Kurosawa, Godard, Tarkovsky, or Reiner used to make me feel bad – guilty, even. It would turn a hobby into a chore, and lagging behind is rarely fun. Not to mention that in this respect, complete familiarity with masters, past and present, is an absurdly unattainable goal.

But I have time yet, I have my twenties to get started, to remind myself that all of the expectations I hold for myself are particularly unrealistic given how little time I have devoted to this corner of the art world.

The classics have waited this long – they can wait a little longer. Nineteen-year-old me is off the hook.

The hope I see is of something distant.

I hope that, one day, in the great individuality of my twenties, I will see the criticism I already levy against the whole 'generations' matter as something to embrace.

Sticking out, but more specifically, sticking out from

the norm I perceive other people to have set, is currently my nightmare. But the roadmap I crave, those boundaries I find comforting now, are bound to show the dangers of their limits eventually.

The sooner I can progress from recognising that fact to accepting it, the better.

In a *Variety* conversation with actor Bryan Cranston, *How I Met Your Mother's* Jason Segel said, 'You spend your twenties trying to get somewhere, like I'm on the road to there,' but that it wasn't until his thirties that he had 'this realisation that there is no *there*, right, this imaginary *there*, it just keeps moving equidistant away from you'.

What he realised three or four years ago was that he needed to 'find a model that is sustainable' – one to allow for not feeling like he's 'in a state of waiting for this thing to happen – you're in it right now'. Now doesn't feel like much, but that hope extends to a future now, in which it feels like *everything*.

I am on the cusp of twenty-hood, of no longer being a teenager.

I have, as T.S. Eliot put it, 'nor youth nor age'. On the occasions that I do find myself 'dreaming of both', I imagine them not as what they were or are, but what they could be.

They could be anything.

They could be everything.

Characters, Take One

When I used to teach creative writing, I would tell the students to make their characters want something right away – even if it's only a glass of water. Characters paralyzed by the meaninglessness of modern life still have to drink water from time to time.

Kurt Vonnegut

SHE ASKED HIM where he was. He asked her where she wanted to be.

'Here, with you.'

He opened his eyes and looked at her, standing by the window. The light of day was unremarkable, the world did them no favours. The only occasion was each other's company.

She looked for him out there, her eyes finding momentary detail and rest in the city that was theirs. There was a billboard for a show he once told her he thought she'd like, a woman in a sundress of the same red-and-white polka-dotted pattern as the boxers he was wearing now, a student carrying takeout from that Mexican joint he liked because it was the only place where he had a 'usual'.

She turned.

He stretched.

She had class in twenty minutes.

He was already late for his.

She watched him dress, and helped him find his keys.

They both walked downstairs, stepping into the morning's inviting air.

He was used to thoughts he didn't understand. His mind was an agent of uncertainty – he could feel how fast it was spinning, but he could never quite tell where it was, exactly.

With her, his feelings weren't thought, they were projected into his muscles and onto his skin. She could turn him from an empty fog into a storm cloud.

His life was words, his sanity predicated on a belief that enough of the right ones, in the right order, were the purest instruments of change. Some words meant more to him because of her. There were those he had never doubted, and the rest he knew came to mean some version of her.

Home was the tender security she made him feel. *Dread* became hers when she was running late for their second date. She had become meaning to him, all he was and knew he had trusted to her care.

That's something I'm working on. It's Timur speaking (writing?), by the way.

I don't see the point in stalling, holding out for a possible future – a future in which all the work I release into the world is perfectly crafted. So, consider this a loose page from a sketchbook, complete with construction lines, eraser-smudges, and attempts and embryonic ideas. Actually, it might be more apt a comparison to call this a sandbox, in which anything can be created, there are no stakes, and everything is a mess from the start.

In the spirit of my writing not being at its best, I am happy to admit my current limits. Writing fiction is not something at which I excel. Every part of writing that I enjoy, of sitting in front of a keyboard and stringing words together, is placed at a higher barrier to entry when I'm writing fiction.

I've so far managed to squeeze by with what can quite simply be described as 'transcribing my stream of consciousness'.

My thought-stream doesn't regularly take the shape of a story, complete with fleshed-out plot and character. Tapping into that vein, then, throws a hurdle between me and my otherwise unfiltered output.

There is, of course, one foolproof method by which to get better at something...

To do it more often.

And so I have done, and in the stead of any skill, I have gained a little insight into where exactly my faults lie. To begin with, I don't have the patience for it. Yes, it is quite simple, as the fact is there is little more tedious and unrewarding to write as something I have planned out in my mind already.

Besides the myopic redundancy, I think it also reveals how much my appreciation for writing comes from the feelings of cleverness and accomplishment that appear to go well with the tendency of mine to print my thoughts as I think them – raw, though still curated.

Another internal issue stifling the output of my fiction writing is the unreliability with which I am able to produce, then develop, sound ideas. I have a frustratingly high bar, and yet a low tolerance, for story prompts or plans, especially those that seem a bit too familiar, or that don't meet my indefinable originality and excitement thresholds. But, mirroring an earlier point, the process of trying to develop a plot makes me feel dumb.

Resolved as I appear to be to attempt this skill growth with no help from outside resources, it can be demoralising when an intrinsic facet of fiction writing calls for something for which I have never held a good track record.

As I read the work of others while attempting my own, it seems as though I'm wearing glasses with special lenses – lenses that enable me to glimpse behind the curtain.

I know how the sentences were written.

I know why they haven't introduced dialogue yet.

I know they avoided using this word two pages ago because it's punchier here.

I can recognise all these signs, but I can't produce any of my own.

So far, with fiction, I've had to settle for mimicry, desperate for a morsel of inspiration to latch on to.

But then, there's something else I can try.

The only reason I want to write what I deem 'good' fiction is that it seems to offer limitless perspective and scope to thoughts, those that originate from a mind that feels painfully constricted by comparison.

The fragment of a story you would have read at the outset is, I hope, a first step out of the quagmire in which I dwell.

A piano teacher once spent weeks reinforcing to me the notion that, when studying a piece of music, the trick is to break it down into its smaller constituent parts. Elementary though it may have been, that lesson felt like a piece falling into place – and like a metaphor that can surely serve me as I progress from one form of keyboard to another.

A last reason why writing fiction is a challenge for me is because of characters. Constructing one that feels real has never been my forte. In every half-decent piece of fiction I've ever produced, the characterisations contained within are far from original. While I may be bad at characterisation – even when it is based on myself or someone I know well – on a general level, my shortage of skills is definitely at its most apparent whenever I try to remove those traces of me.

So, consider this a test.

I'm trying to recreate the sandbox – building real things that I can mess up or even break without too much worry.

Break it down.

All I need to do is produce any amount of plot, planning, patience, and character, and make sure the product is something I am content with, something my inner critic wouldn't be too hard-pressed to call 'good'. Proving to myself that this is something I can achieve in any amount at all is a lesson I think it would do me good to learn.

In addition to embracing and slowly moving past failure, I must remember that the best results will come from being deliberate and intentional, and not hoping to stumble onto a right answer and be able to move on.

Progress will be slow and it will be painstaking.

But I'll live. I'll be better for it.

Where Do I Go To?

To be sensual, I think, is to respect and rejoice in the force of life, of life itself, and to be *present* in all that one does, from the effort of loving to the breaking of bread.

James Baldwin, *The Fire Next Time*

I AM AT least fifteen seconds away.

In every moment of my life, my focus and attention are concentrated and scattered in every which way but this one. I am in the future, hoping for, or merely existing in, another time.

When the past envelops me, I am one with and succumb to the feeling it brings.

In the timeless, I am nothing but separate, a distinct other from myself.

Aware that the actual clinical term refers to a psychiatric condition, I am hesitant to use the word 'dissociate'. I open myself up to any psychological diagnosticians who seek to admonish, or make sense of my paths of thinking. And, in lieu of a term I feel can accurately describe the mental state which I intend to discuss, I'm going to go with 'faux dissociation'.

Another thing to disclose is that I have absolutely no idea which portions of myself are me and which are just features of the standard human mind.

That said, I am my own favourite subject, and so won't rest until every banal corner of my probably off-the-shelf mind has been somewhat rationalised to myself and communicated with words and sentences far longer than is strictly necessary.

Most people my age haven't, I imagine, scrubbed their mind for content, made sense of it and translated it into forced, inelegant prose.

My sympathy lies with the ones who have.

To put the first paragraph simply, I struggle to 'live in the moment'.

Writing about the present forces me into it.

But yes, that wishfully charming aphorism that I associate with nothing less than the most milquetoast members of the human population raises a once-interesting point for me – and does little else.

I bring all this up for two reasons:

First, to dissect this behaviour of mine until I reach a sad, deflated conclusion, and then to try and disprove that conclusion if necessary and possible.

What I mean by not living in the moment might seem to be quite a neutral practice, but it's one I fear is costing a lot of free enjoyment of the present. It refuses to spare me from anxiety as it pertains to my future, and keeps me from accessing the length and breadth of my mental and emotional faculties.

How this manifests in my real life is that it takes a small but concerted effort to draw focus away from the past or future, and onto myself and, crucially, what I'm doing. What I'm actually doing could be anything, and therein lies what I hope is the central point: I could be working, worrying, relaxing, or simply thinking.

Without that present-mindedness, so too am I bereft of quality in carrying out those aforementioned verbs, or indeed, any others. That work would take twice as long as necessary, and be half as good at best.

That worry would concentrate a feeling of uneasiness in me without a possibility of escaping to some reasoned respite. Even relaxation removes me from taking notice of the enjoyment I seek. Chiefly, though, being unable to think with my wits is what demonstrated the unfortunate harshness of this all.

It may seem excusable to have one's thoughts somewhere else when carrying out a task; those excuses quickly run out when the task exists in one's own head.

Being 'present' for the act of thinking seems like it should be a given.

It isn't.

It feels less like having my thoughts far away when I should be doing something else, and more as if I am existing in another, or no, place in time. It's always a skewed version of time, too, a past that didn't happen quite how I remember or a future I have no way of knowing will come to pass.

It may carry on as a theme from my faux dissociation to refer to this as 'proto-hallucination'. They have a dreamlike realness, where what is seems natural and how it has always been, where questions need not be asked and action need not be taken. They carry no plot or any narrative, but push me into a state of being that is different, often so much more pleasant than the one I have no idea I'm no longer inhabiting.

So, no, I can't live in an actual present moment.

But I can live in others.

Verbs exist in the past, present, and future, but they take refuge, too, in more lateral domains. And it is from those in-betweens – the pasts within pasts and uncertain futures, with those wisps of candid thought – that I ultimately return.

Never when in them do I notice that I am, but I am instead treated to memory of wrenching back the autonomy of my mind as I exit this proto-hallucination. And with a tug from my synapses, I grasp the stark differences between what is and what simple beauty my mind told me was.

It is as if my mind in its most 'natural', thinking state is a blank sheet of canvas, upon which some invisible pencil scrawls letters and words – legible and illegible, fleeting and permanent.

As I enter the proto-hallucination, warm pastel colours join the fray.

Before I know it, the entire canvas is ablaze with colour and with mood, with no trace of words or sentences, or notions of any kind. There are no shapes, and everything blends effortlessly into everything else. Then, some imperceptible force violently blasts it all away, wiping out the past and leaving on the canvas only the scribbles once again.

The absence of anything – the sheer nothingness – I referred to, as a space visited in my mind almost as regularly as are the past and the present, is different in part.

I don't recognise it, don't recall the experience of it.

Instead, I just know that same action, the aggressive removal of peace, after which all that is left is myself.

There it is, and here we are.

The dejected, deflated conclusion.

But I feel neither of those things.

I'm more aware of myself. I've revealed a story in which I am the protagonist, and the degree to which any of this is true I'm not sure. Perhaps that's what I am doing here – not merely rationalising the banal corners of my psyche, but doing so while entertaining others, and reassuring myself.

The inexplicable, it would seem, is just a good story.

Eight-Ball

One's dignity may be assaulted, vandalized, and cruelly mocked, but it can never be taken away unless it is surrendered.

Michael J. Fox

A FAVOURITE PASTIME of mine is negotiating the balance between high and low self-esteem.

They each refer to specific parts of my outward and inward self, and it's an ultimately destructive endeavour, tallying up points on either side in order to determine which feeling I get to feel about myself.

I am so grateful that I have a different system.

Admittedly, it's not much better, but it does carry with it the added benefit of letting me hold back from examining myself as a whole:

I succumb to delusion.

That last sentence is true in more ways than one.

In this instance, I refer to the process by which I do actually determine the height of my self-esteem: I deliberate and focus on one thing, and however good or bad that one thing makes me feel about myself. In doing so, I extrapolate outwards, allowing that feeling to encompass and embrace me.

An example:

A few days ago, I went to the barber's. My hair grows fast and thick, so the following is a sentiment I am more than familiar with. On this occasion, I wasn't especially pleased with the finished look, but instead of voicing any complaints to the man with the knowledge and tools for how to resolve them, I paid, and expressed gratitude nonetheless.

The reason for feigning pleasure is that I avoid propagating discomfort at all costs.

But a few days have passed now, and it's grown on me – somewhat literally. The hair has filled in a bit on the sides, and no longer makes my head look a stretched trapezium. I think I look good.

And, as a joyous result, I feel good.

But I am aware of my social deficiencies, incredibly so.

Indeed, I agonise over them, eager for solutions, stopgaps, and explanations that could provide protection from verbal skirmishes.

Why I don't currently hold out much hope for those is simple: I'm right. Any time the voice in my head that I think is me pipes up with his simplistic and bleak proclamation of my social failings, and his confidence that there is nothing I could be doing to improve upon my situation, he seems to carry with him a sense of authority that's impossible to refute. In short, he seems right. His ironclad logic and facts come from the source I have always had to believe was unimpeachable: myself.

Here ends the lukewarm defence of myself.

On to the cringe.

It's been at least a week now since we met them here in New York. If we'd come down just a few minutes sooner, the pool table would have been free, and my friend and I probably wouldn't have met them, or spoken with them at all. But such was our luck, and thus were we relegated to sitting on the sofa, hoping the people at the table would notice it was one a.m. and finish their game quickly.

Then in came...

You know what? I'm just gonna quickly establish some aliases now. I'm going to be amending this story in small ways to better illustrate my point, but it bears enough resemblance to reality for me to want to obscure any details or specifics. So, let's call my friend August. Then, of the two girls I was about to introduce you to, how about May and, um, February? Yep, those seem like perfectly reasonable names. Back to it.

They slumped down on the sofa opposite us.

February was high as all hell. She caught August's foreign accent and immediately started with a volley of slurred questions, interspersed with streams of consciousness that trailed off, and uncontrollable giggling.

May, on the other hand, was the designated sober one. She explained how she was keeping an eye on February, making sure she didn't embarrass herself, embarrass someone else, or fall down the stairs.

She was babysitting.

February had come wishing to hear the click-clack of pool balls. It was then that August and I had found ourselves talking to them. It wasn't pretty, but they were.

Looks-wise, I was feeling good about myself – not to be taken for granted. But, anyway, I can't hold a conversation with someone my age to save my life.

Every second of the silence felt almost painful.

Silence, that is, punctuated by shrill giggling.

In such situations, I cling to a conversational partner relied upon to fill the silences. And, while August was still fielding questions like 'Is Europe fuzzy?', thankfully May provided that comfort.

What followed was a fun half hour, in which we all got to know each other and I pulled off the great miracle of not coming across as an awkward weirdo. Thinking as much but still having come across as that weirdo is still very much a possibility, but I'm going to be generous to myself in this instance, and set that interpretation aside.

Everything came to an end when the pool table freed up.

February loudly declared to May that she was in urgent need of nachos.

Giggling, smiles, and goodbyes followed.

August accidentally sunk the eight-ball. There was no hope of ever beating August. It was more of a case of him playing long enough to beat himself.

Looking at that whole experience now, I didn't come off too badly. At worst, I seemed pretty shy. But, in the week since meeting them, all I thought I wanted to do was to ask May out.

I told August, who was immediately supportive, and the unfortunate recipient of no fewer than five laments and messages from me, announcing that 'I've changed my mind' and that 'I can't do this'.

Deep down I have to know I can do this.

I can do this. I can. I can. I can.

After all, we shared a solid conversation but – oh my god, I can't do this.

I was awkward.

I was weird.

She'll be grossed out.

I looked awful that night – just as I look weird now.

Hold on. Let me think about it. The worst thing to happen would be her saying 'no', right?

No!

What really would be the worst thing that could happen is if she were to say 'yes'.

I just don't know how to date.

What would I do?

Where would we go?

What am I actually trying to accomplish here; do I really want to date?

Thinking about it, I guess it's just that I want to have dated.

Past tense.

Then again, I suppose I might actually enjoy it.

I should ask August's opinion again.

I can't trust my *own* opinions.

I shouldn't.

When I do, it infuriates me.

But I really shouldn't.

I've written about how much sense my opinions make – to positive and negative ends, about how easy it is to think more carefully about that sense, and start to break most of it down. But the credibility I'm sometimes able to dissect exists in this weakened state only when I have the mental wherewithal to do so.

It takes constant effort to free myself from my own head-space, and the Herculean task of preventing overthinking itself requires an awful lot of thought.

So much easier is it, then, to relent – to believe what I ought not even think. Although it may be wrong, it seems right. I don't think there's a happy, or even a hopeful, ending to this. I have not made, nor will I make, any commitments to fight this or allow myself the acid comfort of resignation.

All that I can aspire to is a future position… one in which I don't need to put my neurones through the ringer every time I have a decision, or an internal judgement, to make.

Therapy has helped so far, and it's a habit I would like to explore more and more deeply, but I think an equally beneficial thing would be practice – practice for instances such as the ones outlined above to occur more often. This way, I would be forced into situations where making a concerted effort is a more reasonable option, and growth a more realistic aspiration.

I could also aspire to writing clearer prose.

But let's deal with one piece of the puzzle at a time.

Vice

Rivers know this: there is no hurry.
We shall get there some day.

A.A. Milne, *Winnie-the-Pooh*

PATIENCE IS AN overrated quality.

In all its forms, I find the duty it requires practically impossible to inhabit. A contrast to my generally passive demeanour, it is in those moments calling for patience that my thinking shifts into hyper-action. My pulsing mind won't allow me to hold still, or space out.

Instead, it leaves me with no choice but to exist through each excruciating second in gradual, painstaking succession.

I love anthropomorphising my brain, because it feels so wrong in a frustratingly inarticulable way. It's me, of course. And at the same time, it isn't me. In a way it's similar to that annoying habit some people have of referring to themselves in the third person.

Anyway, Timur isn't only talking about patience in the broad, temporal meaning of the word.

Yes, he can't sit still.

Yes, his ability to feel boredom verges on the superhuman.

Yes, this third-person bit is getting old.

Beyond that definition of patience, I struggle when situations necessitate patience for something. I am resigned, if not content, to waste record amounts of my time, but I cannot tolerate my time being wasted by someone else.

Let me suffer for my own choices, not yours, too.

Yes, among the problems I deal with regarding social interaction, my lack of patience plays a significant role. I profess that, though I have dear friends now, in general I still have absolutely no idea how to make friends.

Any steps that occurred toward that happening are gone from my brain. It may seem a tad reductive to try and boil down the practice of friend-making into actionable steps (I'm not always convinced such steps exist), but that is something I crave, to make the process even a little less daunting and nebulous.

Though friend-making may be an imprecise exercise, it seems that an inescapable aspect of it is the simple act of spending one's hours in the company of a potential friend. It can, then, be a task when I project high hopes and even higher standards upon them. My friends are people I hold extremely dear, but they are not, of course, without their idiosyncrasies. My stream of inconsistent, internal logic manifests as this lack of patience in social situations with strangers.

I feel entirely uninterested in talking to most people, which leads to me doing whatever I can to quit a conversation at the earliest possible stage. And there, the vicious circle in which I exist is revealed, a vicious circle that alternates between an unwillingness and an inability to converse. It would seem that circumstances of the former are excellent training grounds for resolving the latter.

Historically, it's entirely possible for me, in the span of merely a few minutes, to go from one of the following situations to the other:

I could be engaged in a conversation with someone with whom I find no more than superficial interest. Lips tight, stretched into a half-smile, eyebrows slightly furrowed, an expression suggesting an intent focus on my part, masking the constant internal monologue.

That monologue is rattling through reasons I don't want to be listening to this individual, and how I'm desperate for an escape hatch. From that, I might excuse myself, fiddle with some props – like fixing a drink for myself or saying I need to slip off to the loo.

Returning, then, in the ardent hope of starting afresh with someone else.

And I do.

And – holy crap – they're interesting.

And funny.

And I can't really do anything but ask surface-level questions as they answer, with my lips in a tight half-smile, and my brow slightly furrowed.

I'm a one-trick pony, and in desperate search of my second trick.

Unlike a lot of my social deficiencies, though, this one bears a hint of a solution, albeit a distinctly unsatisfactory one:

Grin and bear it.

While others may be able to, I certainly can't shake this as a compulsion without putting in the hours. In this instance, though, I think I can absolve myself of blame. In recent years, I've not had much consistent interaction with people my age. So, whether or not I would have jumped at such opportunities, there were few to go around.

But that will change soon.

And it means if this is still as relevant in a year as it is right now, I can place the rest of that blame squarely back on me.

You may be wondering whether that wraps up my woeful relationship with patience, but there's one more example...

Writing. Notably, writing fiction.

Non-fiction is a muscle I've worked out and trained, but the same is not true for fiction. My fiction-writing physique is still feeble, because I don't have the patience to put it through the paces.

When writing a piece such as this, I'm constrained by one thing – by the speed with which I can think. I already think like I write (or write like I think, depending on your perspective), so I encounter fewer creative bottlenecks.

With fiction, though, the variability of how fast I think is my recurring concern. Since I am incapable of planning anything in terms of story or plot, I tend to come up with most of what I write on the fly – for better or worse.

As much as I feel I could benefit from the organisation of ideas and thoughts that come with writing fiction, it entails, for me, long periods of mental stagnation, during which I can't summon the creative nous to write a compelling next sentence, or work out where the plot ought to be going.

Then something will click, and I'll sense the shape of an idea.

But, instead of developing that idea while writing, I'll think and think, until I know the idea well enough to put it in writing.

And so begins the greater problem.

Having devoted so much bandwidth to that one idea in such a short period of time, I become uninterested in it. I get bored – I've lost all patience with the idea, exhausted at the thought of having to work into being that which already exists whole cloth in my head.

The result leaves me disheartened, and with little work – if any – to show for it.

The solution to this is a single notion, the same one required to counter a lack of social patience.

Just practise. I dream of the fiction space, but it will be a while before I commit to creating in it – creating both successes and failures.

In the meantime, I could benefit from spending more time in the real world.

Assume brace positions.

The Island of
a Misfit Boy's Thoughts

The first draft is just you telling yourself the story.

Terry Pratchett

'HE TASTED HER tears to tell if they were authentic.'

What? Why?

I'm full of sentences like that which need not ever see the light of day. Some are no more than clusters of words. Individually, they don't warrant any further observation or discussion, but hoping they stay hidden in whichever notes app I've buried them in, rather than addressing the collection as a whole, seems a waste.

Like Frankenstein's monster visiting the Island of Misfit Toys – or, if you'd prefer, a metaphor that makes sense, consider this an experiment to deduce whether there is a sum of any value to be found among the scraps.

'It capsized my day.'

Turns out, I have little more to say of my experience kayaking than that it was often a negative experience. But those feelings would always muddle themselves and refrain from hitting me with blinding clarity until the hours or minutes until I actually had to do it. Of course, possessing upper-body strength would have helped, or an affinity for cold-weather water sports.

Oh, to have known better.

We're starting off easy here, though, because I really tried to make this one work.

Capsize my day.

It sounded so cool. Evocative.

A perfect balance of punch and purpose.

A day after my brain had strung it together was the first time I read a piece by Joan Didion; I actually read like five, so drawn was I to her prose.

In her writing, I found her perspicacity, her beautiful melding of wholly different concepts and ideas, utterly enchanting.

Didion described winter as having a 'thin sunlight', and marriage in Las Vegas as 'a game to be played when the table seems hot'. All of it gave an impression of effortlessness in her writing that she reveals never existed. In the preface to *Slouching Towards Bethlehem*, she wrote:

'...all of them were hard for me to do, and took more time than perhaps they were worth.'

But I can't see the construction lines – scribbles in the margin, sentences she crossed out and rewrote. Instead, like everyone else, I'm presented with the finished product. The work as she wanted it to be seen – a finished piece of art.

Only now am I faced with a similar task, one which requires me to peer into a misshapen ball of clay, searching for form and structure.

That contentedness, in comparison, seems a lofty goal. Especially when indifference and resignation rule my thoughts without oversight.

'No one can call it quits like I can.'

This was an outtake that existed as a cool, quippy line, but within the confines of my mind. As soon as it had been translated into this written version of reality, I lost faith in it.

It felt a little sad for my liking. They can't all be winners.

'I am waiting to have a life I can reflect upon.'

A winner, meaningful and succinct.

A victim, unfortunately, of its own success.

There was a time when, as a result of a long stretch of essays I had read, so much of the world I perceived was one seen through other people's eyes. While I spend my time writing about myself, these prosaic pros were examining, dissecting, and reflecting upon their lives.

Curious to notice, the difference between me and my life. Between my life and theirs.

In a glorious way, the perspective with which I observed things no longer had to be the object of my writing in and of itself. Instead, it could be fashioned into the tool with which I could probe for my own insight.

A victim of its own success because it said everything I needed to say.

That's not entirely true, actually – but rather me being defensive. I admit, it captured my point in its entirety, just while not saying everything I wanted it to.

And the reason it won't is that I felt as though any attempts to elaborate or expand that thought, to relate it to myself in a personally significant way, would be diminishing.

But I like it.

I really do.

If not only for the truth I maintain it conveys, but for the potential it represents, too. It speaks of a time in which I may be prepared to reflect meaningfully at length about an equally lengthy life. Or, perhaps, a time in which my writing abilities and confidence have been elevated sufficiently for me to articulate exactly why I feel incapable of genuine reflection.

'One tomorrow at a time.'

I really liked this one, and I still may use it, but its absence from any of my current work is as simple as it is personally amusing. I hate coming up with unoriginal ideas; I much prefer to copy from myself. This is a behaviour I often exhibit in extremes, to the detriment to how much I enjoy that idea or believe I could do it justice.

One finds oneself, then, constantly shifting between the poles of something excitingly original that a few people have used, and an idea so heavily used it easily edges itself into cliché.

The healthy medium is so rare, but there is a fortunate result of going through periods of time in which I project every negative adjective onto my work, and think little to nothing of my abilities as a writer. Simply, it is that it makes the clichés seem less of a shameful choice and more of a resigned allowance for myself.

Resignation fuels a not insignificant portion of my creative output.

This example, though, of taking something – life, perhaps – 'one tomorrow at a time' was one I relished. It felt refreshingly original for me. Yet, equally, it was one I correctly believed had already been used. It's the title of a song by an artist called Josephine Genais. And, although I had expected a result such as this, I was still a little bitter.

So, I listened to the song to see if I could learn to hate it. But I liked it.

It's simply a good song, and I added it to my library before I even finished hearing the full thing.

I was happy, and she used the phrase in a way completely unlike how I would have.

The moral of the story is obvious – there's never anything new under the sun.

What I did find surprising, though, was that in this instance, resignation suffered a rare defeat against positivity: the kinship I felt in a brief parasocial relationship – that imagined kind of tether between myself and someone who doesn't even know who I am – all with an artist for whom I claim a personal connection no more substantial than a song title.

Considering it, I should try coming up with ideas more often, because I bet I can score myself a better resignation-to-weird-version-of-a-positive-experience batting average.

'He tasted her tears to tell if they were authentic.'

I'd like to return to this one for a moment, because I felt awkward ending on that fragment of sincerity; and because the reason I decided not to use this line is as laughable as it is senseless.

You see, I used the wrong word.

Every other day or so, I consider writing a completely new type of piece. Then, right away, I reconsider when I remember where I feel my abilities lie, and what I actually enjoy writing. Some ideas get further than others. This one got pretty far, and it started with that sentence.

What I had in mind was a proto-sci-fi short story.

One of the characters (or a bunch of people, I didn't spend

much time fleshing it out) would taste someone's tears to see if the supposed emotion that caused them was real, or if they were being faked. I had this cool, weird image in my head of a jealous person forcefully grabbing their weeping partner's face to judge whether the tears were, indeed, the result of overwhelming emotion.

The word I was looking for was 'genuine', but I had used 'authentic'. Like they were tears that someone else had given their stamp of approval. Anyway, by that point, the damage was already done.

From the moment I really started picturing it, it was impossible for me to stop seeing it as a dystopian noir film aspiring to third-rate writing. One in which a third-rate detective solves third-rate murders by interrogating random people roughly, then rushing to lick their faces when they start to cry.

It didn't make any sense at all.

It was so stupid.

But it was an image that got trapped in my head.

Perhaps I'll return to that line one day.

Or to the one about a life to reflect.

Or to the one about tomorrows.

Or to the one about capsizing my day.

Or, hell, even to the one about calling it quits.

Or to the dozens of others I've forgotten about.

Yes, I am sure I shall return to this island, but no longer out of desperation.

It's a realm of possibility. Turns out, that's a pretty cool thing.

Seemed Neater

For last year's words belong to last year's language
And next year's words await another voice.

T.S. Eliot, 'Little Gidding', *Four Quartets*

WHEN I FIND a way to describe myself that I think is catchy, I stick to it.

It becomes the default answer both to questions I'm asked, and questions I ask myself. It's rarely a complete untruth, but whatever percentage of verity it once contained is at its greatest at the descriptor's conception.

That is when it will be the most true.

What happens, then, as time goes on, and my faith in it declines, is that I will look for things that prove it right. It makes me at least a little more comfortable to know that I'm trying not to lie to myself and others.

Eventually, I have to let it go.

The phrases that last become a pair of things in their lifetimes: slivers of thoughts I once clung to, in an effort to define at least part of my identity, and symbols of my love for words.

I used to like describing myself as an 'aspiring optimist'.

But, in the years since it seemed to fit me so well, I've outgrown it.

I can remember the person who thought it was right. He loved the pair of words 'aspiring optimist', and was so protective of that 'creation', and the way it resonated with him, that he didn't want to risk researching its originality.

As far as he wanted or needed to know, it was his and his alone.

It fit so well with the worldview he felt it right to espouse, that he could be his own kind of happy-go-lucky optimist. At the same time, however, he could wear the word 'aspiring' as armour to protect him from potential accusations of stagnation, and claiming an attempt, or desire, to change.

There was, though, a word that he knew described him better.

He loathed it – for it painted a picture of him, ugly and true-to-life.

He was sort of delusional. I sort of still am.

I tend to twist thoughts towards the negative. So, when I've found myself conflating the definitions of 'optimism' and 'delusion', the one I related to more, the one that felt more self-critical and correct, was 'delusion'.

To me, the combined ideas of optimism and delusion whispered of an imagined future, implicitly good, or containing a precious morsel of good news. With no reasonable basis upon which I could attach any sense of realism to either future, I defaulted to a less generous one.

It derived from an unwillingness to corrupt my optimism.

That's what I felt would happen, if one of these imagined futures didn't come to pass.

I chose the descriptor of 'delusional' to prevent my loss of faith in optimism, to prevent the latter from becoming completely synonymous with the former.

It wasn't and isn't forgiving.

Optimism stales when confined to futures built on probability and certainty.

I don't want to come across as pitiable here, because I'm

really not. Allowing myself an image of a good thing, without having to ask the questions that may shatter the façade, has been encouraging and even empowering. It's birthed a different negative tendency, though, and it's one I am trying to nip in the bud.

In addition to the general delusion and pessimism I preferred to refer to as 'realism' exists my great capacity to fixate. *How I Met Your Mother*, which as you know by now is one of my favourite shows of all time, is home to several quotes that constantly rattle around my head.

Only one, though, is relevant here.

Ted and Marshall, the protagonists, have been best friends since college. They live in an apartment on New York's Upper East Side, and are playing video games, when the subject of the apartment itself comes up. Marshall is engaged to his college girlfriend Lily, and the question is who'll get the apartment once they've tied the knot.

Most days, the following exchange pops into my head at least once:

[Flashback]

Marshall: So when Lily and I get married… who's gonna get the apartment?

Ted: Wow, that's a tough one. You know who I think could handle a problem like that?

Marshall: Who?

Ted: Future Ted and Future Marshall.

Marshall: Totally. Let's let those guys handle it.

[Present Day]

Ted: Dammit, Past Ted!

I'm caught between that pair of states, the two timelines: worrying about the future and then, not planning for it. How comforting it would be to relate to just one, but I have an all-too adversarial relationship with Future Timur.

I try to ignore him and, as a result, he resents me.

Be it inaction or generally poor choice of action, I invariably choose the course of events more likely to make his life more inconvenient. It's easy to think of him like this, as a person quite different from myself – if only so as to alleviate the guilt I'd feel at having inconvenienced myself.

That's the first half of the equation.

While doing all this to aggravate Future Timur, I take my share of his problems. They toe the unfortunate line of occupying my mind and appearing to be without clear solution. That's an outcome I find almost criminally offensive – an unclear solution. They rob me of any possible sense of comfort or accomplishment.

All of this is why I fixate.

When good news or a solution presents itself, my brain has the frustrating habit of replacing it with whatever was next on my list of worries. In which case I defer to those of Future Timur. Together, we have at our disposal an endless supply of bad to replace the good, worries to put the successes in a disappointing context.

This has long been a flowchart by which my thought processes have operated. By which I have operated.

Since most changes in my behaviour have passed with no effort on my part, I am grateful for the one that has begun to crop up. Those worries upon which I spend so much of my time fixating are usually beyond my control; or are decisions with seemingly no perfect outcome.

In instances of the former, I do my utmost to engage ignorance in all its blisses. But, in matters where perfection becomes my unwieldy goal, it is this idealism that I focus my efforts on subduing.

In the offices of quality that reside inside my skull, there is a building marked 'Just Fine'. In a sub-sub-basement, in a forgotten broom closet, sits Perfection, bound and gagged, and I am safe from his discomforting pleasures.

Safe, at least, for a little while longer.

Unless You

To think too much is a disease.

Fyodor Dostoyevsky, *Notes from Underground*

IT TOOK ME a long time to grasp the fact that having a best friend isn't necessarily a mutual condition. Nor is it something requiring equal reciprocation.

The fact used to sadden me.

And it still does, sometimes.

In ways stretching from my attitudes to others, to my writing, to attitudes towards myself, perspective has always eluded me. The thought, then, that I could hold one person in such high esteem, feel a trust, comfort, and devotion, was a thought I viewed through a pinhole, blackness surrounding it, blackness obscuring the larger picture.

What lies beyond that picture was not – is not – a solution to my lack of perspective. Because a picture is perhaps a clearer metaphor than pinhole; the shallow depth of field retaining one part of the image in focus, while the colours and shapes around it serve as little more than suggestions.

The thing about such shallow depictions of the world is that the subject is, by necessity, small. In the same way good photography can be enlivened with a story, my responses to truths that aren't wholly positive could only be more personally productive, and even healthy, if injected with more detail.

This is a complicated way of saying that, just because I considered someone my best friend, my assumption they felt the same way fails to take into consideration the life and sentiments and experiences of that whole other person.

Myopia is a problem I'm working on.

Or, rather, it's a problem I want to have worked on.

None of this would be as definitive a self-admonishment if it all weren't such a mainstay of my emotional memory.

As nebulous a gamut as emotion is, the attachment of specific combinations, specific cocktails of feelings, are the most potent kinds of memory. The thought that my friends may not care about me at all made for a particularly nasty blend that I felt content to put back on the shelf in my mind, where time and dust could dull me to it.

Every day since entering my teens, since the pie chart of my mental faculties became increasingly dominated by the process of overthinking, results have rarely skewed towards the good.

Shakespeare may have been right when he wrote in *Henry V* that, 'in peace there's nothing so becomes a man / as modest stillness and humility'.

But peace and humility and stillness, much less a singular good, are all completely foreign to me, and I know that I am the poorer for it. Overthinking isn't one of the extremes in which one can exalt in the excess.

It's something of which to be wary, something which oft makes me weary.

Too much thought drives me to inaction.

So does too little thought, but the kind of inaction that overthinking works into being is cold and acerbic, a *powerless* form of inaction. The kind that finds yearning, a desire to act somewhere in the mind, and tells you why you can't fulfil it, why it would be ultimately ruinous to fulfil it.

My friends know this now.

Now.

My explaining it to them, or their having to point it out to me inquisitively, were individually uncomfortable. But so, too, were they reliefs. It was as though I'd had a broken leg as long as I'd known them, but they finally could see and accommodate a crutch – and help, if not treat me.

When my overthinking seeped into the perceptions of my friendships, I experienced fear blended in with that powerlessness. I knew that, left to its own devices, it would corrode my sense of trust, dismantling something I considered integral and precious.

Thank god my friends didn't let it, then.

The one real antidote deployable against overthinking is *deus ex machina*.

Once my overthinking latches onto its prey, the only thing which can pry open its grip is the subject itself, confronting the work of overthinking head on.

Some instances are inevitable.

I had overthought and stressed myself out to an excruciating extent about a course on which I was due to participate last year. But experiencing what it actually turned out to be dissolved that notion.

Concepts are trickier.

So when a friend called me two days ago, with the weight of the world on his mind and no good feeling in his body, something inside me shifted. As I listened, doing my best to comfort him, I couldn't help but feel validated.

Since what followed was a frank discussion of our mental health, I raised that exact point with him. Putting the validation into words, he quashed my overthinking.

This was a very selfish take, and I recognise that, but he addressed that himself when he told me that helping someone didn't need to be an active thing – just being there can count.

So, that's what we both did.

And yes, the ninety minutes we spent talking, and I spent pacing around a carpet as is my customary phone call behaviour, was not easy, but perfect. It was in my parents' bedroom in my childhood home, which felt really fitting.

A past version of myself, one which had existed in and around that room, was a stranger to overthinking, but not a stranger to being comforted. The environment in which my friend and I met and bonded was far less conducive to connecting over such vulnerability.

A meeting of those two worlds and times, as that phone call represented, was simply beautiful.

Inaction, then, doing nothing, *just being there*, will be something good.

Something I can choose to do.

If nothing else, that experience and the realisation that sparked this piece foretell that there is to be more such connection in my future. That future will no doubt be when my emotional memory is more ripened, and my presently even-handed struggle with overthinking is one that I'm winning.

Or, better still, my bane finally is down for the count.

Curating My Memory

If you wish to forget anything on the spot,
make a note that this thing is to be remembered.

Mark Twain

We tend to keep our distance, my memory and I.

Unsurprisingly to those who know me, I like to think of my memory as an oracle, as one might find in any of the famous Greek myths.

Personal, confusing, it's built to be unreliable and to portend what's still to come. But all that discussion is itself still to come, as I must start with a confession:

I have a terrible memory.

The truth is that I can't really rely upon it consistently. I just don't trust it.

It's not always bad, but following a lesson I've picked up from those same Greek myths, I do my best to try to avoid direct consultation with my own inner oracle.

As I traverse the depths of my memory, back through months and years, the gaps widen and, increasingly, I see asterisks.

I had an unconventional childhood in Morocco and in India, before attending a boarding school lost in the English countryside. I don't know if these lapses in memory are consequences or symptoms of, or even at all related to, that childhood, but it's a correlation that is hard to ignore.

Before the age of fourteen, I have mental snapshots – still images captured of a place or a moment. But the harder I try and focus on those, to expand them to glimpse more detail, the hazier the edges become. Before I know it, they have faded into unreliable and superficial reflections, estimations of experiences lived long ago.

It wouldn't take me long to enumerate the actual events of my early childhood, the ones that I can honestly recall. They constitute half of my living memory. The rest is home to those pesky asterisks, not to be trusted because of the stories.

The stories that exist as my father's anecdotes and exaggerations, and my mother's quips and reflective comments, as video footage and audio tracks, and as books in which I make a passing appearance.

Curiously, my sister doesn't exist in the asterisk section, but as a mutual participant.

An ally of sorts, she is not quite as blank a slate as me. My sense is that we were on a level enough playing field to register, and indeed to process, memories together.

Most of this wouldn't naturally bother me – I have forged a life around this malformed memory, but I'll get to that in a bit – if it weren't for an insidious by-product of this whole mess.

In her book *The Writing Life*, Annie Dillard put into words the quote about which I think perhaps the most often, that 'how we spend our days is, of course, how we spend our lives'.

It had a rather profound effect on me.

So simply, Dillard was able to lend every single moment that passes for us the magnitude and reverence we so rarely do. We are humble averages – neither defined by the greatest nor by the most heinous thing we have ever done, but by the mundanities that occupy the space between.

And so, ostensibly, it shouldn't really bother me that most of what I've forgotten from my childhood are the in-between moments. Time travel, as it has been present in media, has long suggested that any small action carried out in the past could have wide-ranging consequences for the future. But that's not how people are accustomed to thinking about the presently inconsequential.

As Dillard submits, those seemingly mundane experiences are as conducive to our lives and identities as are the more bombastic, memorable ones.

Once broken down, those moments begin to feel decidedly less trivial.

From the routines I lived in but cannot recall, to the habits I tried to shake, to my hobbies, to the conversations I exchanged with friends.

My friends.

The person I am today is shaped just as much by my having had close friends throughout my childhood as it is by the fact that I remember close to nothing about any of those friendships.

Although this isn't an essay about my social connections, I do want to touch on them. It might be no more than correlation, but around the time my memory proper began to form, the earliest instances of my social anxiety occurred, too. It can be frightening for me to think about the fact that as soon as I started to develop a strong sense of self, it revealed to me what I have since perceived as varying degrees of a character flaw.

I can tie this back to memory.

A significant factor in my social anxiety is the fact that I neither really know how to make friends, nor do I really know how I have done so in the past. I have around a dozen close friends about whom I care greatly, and whose opinions I value an equal amount.

It may just be another one of my catchy descriptors, but I have absolutely no idea how we became friends.

With most of them, I have enough of an established rapport that I know how to carry myself around them, and can generally be close to my real self. Yet I don't know the steps that went into making that the case and, man, I wish I did.

Because if I did, I wouldn't feel as out of my depth as I so often do when meeting new people. Nor would I have to moderate myself so much to fit in. I can remember the good times and the bad times I've shared in the company of my friends, but there's an inexplicable lack of control felt in almost every other moment, every moment in which my memory has had a hand.

Beyond that, the disappointment I feel around failing to remember my friends before boarding school is about more than its effects on my current sociability. It's about the fact that I know I have had meaningful relationships with others, relationships that clearly meant enough for me to be able to recall the veneer of it all, but any actual substance is irrevocably lost.

If how I spent my days back then was, even in part, connecting with these other people, then that part of my life is missing, and I am left only to guess at what it might have been, and the various ways in which it has shaped who I am now.

American essayist Ralph Waldo Emerson wrote that '[he] cannot remember the books [he has] read any more than the meals [he has] eaten; even so, they have made [him]'. As comforting an aphorism as I have found that in the past, and continue to do, it is undeniable that I feel a sort of wistfulness in knowing that so much of what has made myself is lost to me.

I'll admit that it's not only the memories I'm missing that frustrate me, but it's so much easier to point my anger in their direction than to address the larger fact of my eroding trust in the ones that remain.

I've mentioned the asterisks, the influences I have undeniably succumbed to in the formation of my memories, but there is one other kind I left out. This one is less an issue of compromising the memory than it is of a questionable retrieval system.

Humans are extremely fond of stories.

They encompass our lives from the art we create to the art that we consume, but it goes a level deeper. So affected are we by stories that we feel such a desperation to be in them, and to find them in ourselves.

I'm sure the field of psychology has proved as much, though the rest of what I have to say on the matter is based on nothing more than my own, isolated experience.

It starts with my love of movies.

It's that simple.

I absolutely love movies and TV shows, and reference

that fact with great regularity in almost everything I write. Despite this passion – or perhaps as a result – my taste in movies did not stray far from the mainstream until a couple of years ago, when I made it an endeavour of mine to watch and consume *ungodly* amounts of media.

One senses patterns.

One is affected by those patterns, and by more they didn't even know about. I am that one. In the time since beginning that exploration, having exposed myself to cinema from a breadth of genres, and from times and countries vastly different to mine, I've seen a lot of depictions of the human condition. And I've seen personal stories, stories in which the stakes are apocalyptic, stories that are nothing more than a conversation between two characters.

In seeing how people write people, I've come to understand more the narratives and literary devices we find convenient to attach to characters – fictional, real, as well as our own.

Humans are terribly susceptible to co-opting fiction as fact.

Look no further than the ever-prevalent parasocial relationship, in which people find it difficult to unblur the lines between a character as they perceive them in media, and someone they feel they know in their real lives. The same fact is true of politics, of bonds formed at early ages, and of certain kinds of propaganda.

The tantalising and simple-to-form insidiousness doesn't stop at the conviction that something unreal is real, or something untrue is true, but at the 'facts' of such an untruth overwriting and correcting our already malleable, plastic memories. We can remember a crowd jeering because that's the sentiment communicated to us after the fact. And we can remember loving a sibling with whom we spent our formative years in shifting states of dislike.

Those methods of character development are just symptoms of how we like our stories to be told, and what *are* our memories if not fragments of stories we're trying to make whole? We – apologies, *I* – strive to glue those fragments together with logic and familiarity and story arcs, but the truth is often so much more mundane.

Life is one random variable supplanting another in endless succession, and isn't trying to make sense any more than I am successful in trying to anthropomorphise it. I retain pieces of that randomness in my memory, attempt to create a coherence that was never there to begin with, just because it's more comfortable than knowing that very little of what I 'know' means anything at all.

We remain fantastic vessels for stories, and capable of wondrous storytelling. Not only do I think that stories affect our memories, but that the reverse is also just as true.

The earliest form of storytelling existed because of a balance between human creativity and memory. It continues to survive. From the fireside stories of millennia past to the myths that dominated the ancient world, to cautionary tales, to bedtime stories of the modern age, and the deeply engrained thread of narratives present in every culture today.

When the norm came to be established of writing those orations – those stories – down, to preserving them on scrolls or stone, or animal skins, we realised those memories, and made them into artefacts. They were made tangible, and became objects we could protect.

A story was only as good as the memory of its audience.

Quality is an inherently subjective thing, and a story needs both understanding and recollection for any kind of judgement to be placed upon it. Sometimes those memories come short, and a story is changed. And sometimes someone just wants to change it. But, in this endless stream of collaboration that started with early man, and with which we continue to interact, more than a credit can be given to a dodgy memory.

More credit, though, ought to go to the recontextualisation of a memory – be it someone else's or our own – through who we are in the present and what value we feel can be gleaned from it.

At this point, it may seem that I'm merely putting into words every single thought I can summon on the subject of memory. That is partially true, but I'm going to try and focus back again, with reference to something I mentioned at the start – memory as an oracle. At first, it seemed like no more than a pretty metaphor to me, but has proved to have more layers the more I unpack it.

First, another quote.

I have a particular fondness for this one, uttered by one of the many psychedelic characters in Lewis Carroll's *Through the Looking Glass*. The White Queen, speaking to Alice, remarks that 'it's a poor sort of memory that only works backward'.

It resonated with me greatly, as it reflected a belief that until that point, I didn't even know I held – that memories, like oracles, can portend the future. I can be fairly accused of having a failing imagination, but what little vestige of it actually remains I hold as crucial in my pastime of looking to the past and extrapolating forward.

For reasons enumerated, these 'truths' of my future felt just as true as did those of my past. As much as I like the symmetry of that fact, though, it isn't always a good thing.

Now please excuse this planned tangent before I conclude that point:

That realisation of my attachment to truth in my experience arose over recent years, over which I have been making a concerted effort to hold on to my past in various forms, as my memory whimpers on in a corner of my mind. This thankfully tangible (or at the very least, readily accessible) record ranges from the outwardly mundane to the deeply significant. For example, I have a complete history of where I have been, when and for exactly how long, with a visual representation of that and a lot more data to boot.

Some people don't realise their phone can track them, some people do, and make sure to disable the feature, but I consider it a valuable part of my independently sourced memory. Thanks to another helpful gadget, I have no need to recollect how I felt about a night of sleep, and I'm provided with yet more data and helpful charts that my memory only wishes it had up its sleeve.

Moving on to the things I take more seriously: films.

Yet one more symptom of my new and somewhat solid

identity is the solace I take in watching movies. An excuse I've given myself for the inordinate amount of time I've spent watching them is that I do it in order to better immerse myself in the language of narratives and to better equip my linguistic arsenal.

Unlike some of the other nice things I say to myself, this one happens to be true. But it's not the whole truth, of course. Movies are *fun*. They are, in a way, a pinnacle of human creativity. The best ones, with all of their perfectly melding visual and sonic qualities, have the capacity to mesh together in just the right, meticulously choreographed way, to affect their audience.

Clearly, I can gush about films.

That gushing is itself only intensified when a particularly great, or terrible, film is the subject, but to an unfortunate point. I know what my favourite films are, but that's taken more effort to know than one might think.

My memories of films are perfect examples of the true nadir of my memory's abilities. I can usually remember the plot and some set pieces, but I usually set the bar for myself at 'remembering that I have seen the film'.

No opinions, let alone details, are stored, or at least that would be true if I were talking only of the confines of my brain.

That's where Letterboxd.com comes in.

This miracle of a website has served as a repository of all the films I've seen for over four years now. Along with a record of each individual film, I retain the date I saw it, the rating I gave it out of five stars, and the short review I wrote.

This exemplifies something I like about my efforts to actualise my memory – I can compare. I can reliably hold my opinions and thoughts against past versions, and while the improvement is welcome when noticed, I appreciate the ability to observe the change.

It's heart-warming to see the things that were important to me at the time, fleshing out the world of a snapshot, or *creating one where it wouldn't have otherwise existed.*

Which brings me to my pride and joy.

My journals.

Every day since the summer of 2020, I have written a diary entry in tiny script.

Half a page of A5 is the groove I settled into early on in the process, and I have continued it non-stop. It is one of my few good habits, and the one of which I am proudest; partly because it speaks to a small achievement I can claim each day, but mostly because of its function as a storage unit for my memories.

When I sit down to write an entry, I begin the process of reflecting on the day that's just passed – what I did, what I saw, what I felt, and what I thought about.

Once that list has been roughly decided upon, I start putting into words what I would generally like to mention about the day, but more importantly, what I think I'll want to remember.

In this way, I'm forcing my memory's hand.

While I can't claim to agonise over what I'm going to write about, this practice of curation is one I've noticed over time, one that has had some interesting effects. To begin with, it somewhat rewrites the way in which memories are formed.

For the short term, most people have a reasonable expectation to recall with high accuracy the recent events of their lives.

Long term, it's the individually significant or consequential events that remain.

But that's been altered for me.

Sure, the beginning is largely the same: I recount to myself the day's experiences.

What follows, though, is that all that remains is what has been written.

Additionally, the nature of hindsight and the distance of time offer interesting insights to this personal project as it and I grow. Not only are they remarkable, these patterns in behaviour and thought and action that reveal themselves in my writing, but they speak to my outward-facing qualities simply through their existence.

To be honest, this 'curation' of my memories in the journals is less something that I think about every night as I start writing an entry, than it is an undeniable pattern and explanation of myself presented in an obvious, if unintentional way.

I'll see my past the way it seemed important to hold on to.

More and more, then, does that oracle prove its worth.

Kierkegaard wrote that 'life can only be understood backwards; but it must be lived forwards', and that has been made all too clear to me over these past three years. I have noticed repeated mistakes, justifications I am wont to fall back on, consolations I hold too close.

So, will I take the bait, and do just as the oracle says I am to do?

I don't know.

Subtly destructive though they may be, the words of this oracle provide a small comfort of their own, of constancy in the place of growth.

Pourquoi Tu Gâches Ta Vie?

Tu fais n'importe quoi
On dirait que t'aimes ça.

Mika, *Elle Me Dit*

I AM AWARE of my time.

On good days, I value it.

But that mere awareness – comprehension, even – that I exist in an overwhelmingly unlikely transient state called 'consciousness', is not automatically afforded the appreciation that value brings to the table.

And fun though it may be to have one's subconscious remind them of their own mortality, the least pleasant of its effects is a blanketing sensation of guilt at not spending my time the most efficiently for how inescapably temporary it is – for not trying to be the most evolved and accomplished version of myself.

Clearly, I am capable of setting reasonable expectations.

First in my carousel of blame is the overachiever. Though not entirely their fault, the mere existence of those for whom excellence is not a goal but a trophy on their mantelpiece elicits strongly mixed feelings within me.

Positive role models, I am happy to admit, are powerful motivators for individual self-growth, not to mention how empowering trailblazers in certain fields can be to those for whom success is less than a given.

Importantly, I do not seek to invalidate the experiences of such role models nor the countless others whom they have inspired. Instead, the point I would like to establish is one for individuality.

There are numerous successful people in the world whose work ethic got them to where they are, and it's an admirable quality.

But it's not one everyone has.

Nor is it, for those fortunate enough, one that everyone *has* to have.

The reason, though, that I reckon idiots like me think we don't like others excelling is because we live in an age in which excellence is given a platform, and treated almost like a prerequisite to being taken seriously at any level.

Oh, to be a peasant boy growing up in medieval England who would never know the flavour of a Skittle, whose days would be spent in a field, whose life would be lived to exist instead of thrive, who would die at the ripe old age of thirty-six, already a grandparent, but who would never have to know that dozens of people no older than him were surpassing him by every observable metric on a global stage.

The result of that assumed prerequisite, of course, is a unique combination of demoralisation and shame for beholding oneself to the age-old mistake of comparing success or, for that matter, 'successes'.

An equally dangerous part of the success, or excellence, that so much social media and online content comprises, is in the misappropriated value placed on the perfection of the finished product.

We watch experts in their field producing exceedingly impressive content about their particular niches – niches that most people will never know even a fraction as well as the experts do. But what we're really seeing is the latter stage of a much larger-scale commitment made by such experts to familiarise themselves with those niches.

Dozens of examples exist by which I could demonstrate this, from online lockpicking videos to a London taxi driver's addictive YouTube channel, to the endless stream of 'experts react' videos that have developed as their own sub-genre on YouTube, but I'd like to choose a more wholesome case.

Dimension 20 is an improvised comedy TTRPG, a table-top role-playing game, produced and hosted by Dropout.tv, which has executed to a masterful level what may sound like a simple premise. The format is 'Dungeons and Dragons', and the show involves a group of performers, and their unique characters, improvising a story of their own in fictional worlds of varying degrees of fantasy.

Trivial and watershed story-beats alike are decided by the roll of the dice, and the whole game is choreographed – from world-design, to voicing the non-player characters, to ensuring a sense of narrative cohesion – by the game's Game Master.

Brennan Lee Mulligan has served as Game Master for the majority of the various worlds and characters *Dimension 20* has explored in the years since it first began, and the task is no mean feat. It's a fact made all the more frustratingly impressive by the sheer effortless skill with which he manages it.

With a complete command over stories, he uses his background in improvisational comedy to unsurprisingly hilarious effect, and can carry the more dramatic moments with a deft and heartfelt touch. Yes, the job is, essentially, playing a long game with a bunch of his friends, but there's a mountain of work involved that he bears with little apparent struggle.

In a season of the show entitled 'The Seven', one of the player characters was his real-life partner. In a behind-the-scenes look at an episode, she told Mulligan that he makes 'storytelling look easy, which is fucked up because it's really not'. Though expressed in a light-hearted setting, that short, albeit profane, quote speaks to what I find the larger issue here to be.

As an audience, we are rarely privy to the long and tedious process often required to gain mastery of something. Rather, it can be dispiriting to hold as two concurrent emotions an appreciation for the clear skill on display, and a realisation that the chances of my ever reaching that level are slim to none.

Baked into so much of today's 'entertainment' is a sense of the unattainable nature of whatever ideal is being presented. This goes beyond the proliferation of lifestyle-as-entertainment, and has, I think, extended into the subtle conditioning I believe I have undergone to experience the world in such an impersonal way.

Though the internet and social media have given rise to the parasocial relationship – that is, a relationship formed between two people who have never met, one of whom knows nothing of the other's existence – the sheer volume has cast on the whole situation an unfortunately negative glow.

It's all or nothing, and those of us who choose to opt out or find ourselves without, through no choice of our own, can't help but notice the cracks in the content machine.

The digital world has made the banal too skilful and effortful, and created a space where there's nothing one can do that a few taps on social media won't illustrate as already having been mastered and monetised by a stranger.

Perfection exists, and I am not it.

Next up on the already tired metaphor that is my carousel of blame, are value judgements. These are distinct from the sentiment of valuing one's time that I mentioned at the start. Instead, what I mean to say is that there exists – at least in my own experience – stringent expectations that one is spending their time in the best way.

When it comes to productivity, I'm perfectly happy recognising how there are more and less efficient ways to go about achieving it, as well as more and less pleasant ways. But what about fun, and idleness? The issue I take is with the same predilection to optimise being used to create a hierarchy of hobbies and pastimes, of what people do to entertain themselves.

Do I like to read for hours at a time?

Do I like to go on long walks?

Do I like to write for long periods of time?

Do I like to exercise?

YES.

Not always, and not concurrently, but *yes*.

However, do I like to devote half a day to watching movies, television shows, and YouTube videos, or playing video games?

Yes.

I know which ones are better for me than others. But you'd never guess which one gets called an addiction. I did a hundred and fifty push-ups a day for a whole summer. I postponed outings with friends so I could finish my old habit of writing a long, monthly diary entry. I've done nothing for some days but read – and well done me. I've spent consecutive days in front of a laptop screen, having the time of my life.

Wasting one's time is not objective.

Anyway, *for shame*, Timur.

Sometimes, I watch a film like *Eighth Grade*. The directorial debut of comedian/musician Bo Burnham, it's a film whose only intention is to provide humanity to and find beauty in the endless self-consciousness of today's youth. I'm of the opinion that Burnham met and exceeded that goal, and in his writing one can sense the overwhelming empathy; he himself grew in fame and popularity while posting videos to YouTube at age sixteen.

After the film's release, during an acceptance speech for an award from the National Board of Review, Burnham captured in simple words the unfairness I scarcely realised I felt. While I've been trying my best to describe my experience with a symptom, he was able to get to the heart of the disease.

Burnham recognises the false labelling of my generation as 'self-obsessed, narcissistic, and shallow', and brings self-consciousness into the discussion. He questions why 'we are so quick to ask why these kids are looking at their phone all the time, rather than ask what kind of world have we made for them to look up at'.

What I related to most, though, was his stressing that the relationship between the current entertainment and social media landscapes prioritises retention and instant gratification, and that the needs of the children are, as a result, ignored.

Inattention has let this run rampant, and Burnham ends with a suggestion for what a first step would have to look like: 'The answer to their problems, if there is one, is theirs to articulate, not ours.'

The way out of this, the way forward, requires the insight of those at the forefront, and those who currently do, and would have to, deal with the consequences.

I don't pretend that watching the media I do is *always* good for me.

Much of it is junk food for the mind.

But calling it an addiction, and treating it like it's a choice, seems like exactly the wrong combination of things to be doing. Nor is it helpful to pretend that, given the circumstances, any other generation in history would be behaving any differently.

I respect and value safeguarding, which is the least I think Burnham is advocating for in that speech. I also recognise that my generation and the ones to come are, at worst, victims of a system they did not choose – with varying kinds of consequences.

Neither victim-blaming nor mocking the mere existence of victims in this instance is currently needed, because I can guarantee the same people making those 'arguments' would have (a) died for the same entertainment in their childhood that kids have these days and (b) suffered and reacted in exactly the same way.

In case it isn't clear, I did not intend to switch gears to

that message, but I don't regret it. There's nothing quite like an overwhelming feeling of righteous indignation.

I could punch a wall right now.

Ow.

Poems

Poem 1

Conduct my soul you purpose-built
Fear, dreaded – scare me, make me vain,
Slide my self into the silt
Induct me into that which pain
Is followed by – with gentle sputter,
The air is still, no neurones flutter,
It's quiet here beneath the shroud,
Or so your feeling mind does mutter.
What was here before I came?
I left behind a days-old swamp
And have here but the same – the same,
I'm pleased, be proud, my psychopomp.

Poem 2

In water, steam does he go
To life? Mist, it billows inwards,
In a swirling circle of never-end.
Puffing, pulsing, perpetuating him –
A sickening sphere of so-so solid,
Playing hide-and-seek with the cage in his chest.
It rises with him, and with fleeting dive
Abandons and returns to that
Sorry hive of acid mood.
What hums not does it all the same –
Perhaps alive, but life imbued
With mangled pride, open shame.

Poem 3

Alright. Of passage two,
Which lucky one of you
Got any little meaning –
Anything at all that drew
You in a little closer?
Did it speak to something true?
Some cord of understanding,
Banding time-set souls and handing
You a tether – a mortal bond together,
Forged from gut and sinew –
You didn't know it in you
Until all the dust you see
Tiny, solid memory
A lonely I becomes a we
And for its mental tragedy:
Some miserable company.

Poem 4

On the synaptic River Styx
And stony-eyed changers,
Liquid dreams prophetic dangers
Threaten all their ghastly nothing.
What felt once new now feels but spent
Stuck without equivalent.
Wasting it would seem one of the greater
Shames I have carried up with me.
It sits in height and hide and masks its end
In pathetic, fallacious clouds that just portend
A bitter mood, the mind does mend.
But flex and reach and I don't know.
I want to but still I don't know.
I hope and wish, but never know
How much further up it goes.

Poem 5

I'd be a lot less anxious
Nowhere near as pessimistic
If your outright condescension
Showed some cruelty more simplistic
Try and wind its way toward me,
Why would you care to mention,
You know what in life is for me.
And all I do is take your word
And words and words and words and words
And curdle all my insides cuz you silently deterred
Me.

Poem 6

Who stands a chance, my enemy
Inside that slants, my inner me
Against the world, the life I see
Future forgotten memory?
From combinations of word and thought
To conversations since spurred and brought
To oh so many other tables
Originality enables everything short of success
And in that awkward, middle-mess
Of nothing new, and nothing gained,
Lies truly, sorry yours, a heap,
Atrophied with muscles strained
And his sick pride has long since waned
Into his foe – his self doth sleep.
He knows not what those last lines mean,
Nor chose rot, goes jot minds unclean.

Poem 7

Inconsistency is key to
Vexing, motivating me to
Write and wonder what it takes to
Sit down, think up, and make – to
Know within me that to
Want to is the same as to
Create.
Get out of my own way
I say, this time I work, I work away
And mould it, form it, shape it, shine it,
Proud am I – that thing is mine, it
Is me as best I can be
It's rarely me, though. What you see's
A cryptid, a debated life that's
In our mind-timeshare residency.
To be or not to
Be me – the kind of sorry lot to
Dream I'd sieve and filter out my mind to
See what my insides really mean,
Hunt around in there, with fine-toothed
Comb in mental, mental hand. There, scene.

Finis

The Author

BORN INTO A celebrated family of writers and storytellers, Timur Shah has been fascinated with ancient mythologies since early childhood. He was raised at Dar Khalifa, a rambling mansion set squarely in the middle of a Moroccan shantytown, as well as in India, and at boarding school in England.

This is Timur's second book. It follows on from his first – *An Ordered Experience*, which was published to great critical acclaim, when he was nineteen.